Nine Girls
No Boys

Stories Of Life In Rural Virginia

2/20/17

Kay,
Thanks for letting me
share my family's journey with
you. Enjoy!

Daphne

Daphne Harris Dews

Published by BookLocker.com, Inc., St. Petersburg, Florida.

Booklocker.com, Inc.
2017

First Edition

Dedication

Herbert Lee Harris and Annie DeLoatch Harris
(Daddy and Mama).

Acknowledgements

Writing a book requires a great deal of support. I have been fortunate to have the assistance of many individuals—all had an integral part in my completing this project.

I am deeply indebted to my family, especially my sisters—Ruby, Rebie, Minnie, Ernell, Eileen, Yvonne, and Ruth. Their help in recounting and recalling events that took place during our childhood was greatly appreciated. Without them, this book couldn't have been written.

Thanks to my husband James and our daughters, Satonya and Stephanie. They were always eager to read, as well as assist in editing, my writing. Satonya's technological skill was invaluable.

I am so grateful for the support of many of my friends and former colleagues, including Joyce Gilliam Brown, Rebecca Brown, Annie Smith, and Mary Urquhart. They took time to listen, advise, and encourage.

Finally, I want to express my gratitude to members of Virginia Beach Writers. The group provided support that inspired me to seriously consider putting my writings into a book. I want to thank Linda Cobb for her editing expertise, and I especially want to thank the late Ed DeLong, past president of the group, for emphasizing the importance of telling stories of my childhood and insisting that I continue to write.

Table of Contents

THE JOURNEY BEGINS

A man leaves his father and mother and is joined to his
wife and the two are united into one.
Ephesians 5:31

The walk up the lane and steep steps to our grandparents' house seemed to take forever. Daddy's parents lived in a huge farmhouse with a large porch, which stretched across the front of the house. I had swallowed a penny that day, and Mama and Daddy took my sisters and me to their house to get advice on whether or not I should see a doctor.

"Go in the house and talk to your grandma," Mama said, as I approached the front door. "Tell her what you did."
By the time I got to the door and barely inside to greet my grandmother, she knew exactly what had happened. Daddy had already told her. She let him know that since I wasn't having complications, the penny would probably pass through my digestive system in a few days, and I'd be just fine.

Grandma Nora didn't want to hear anything I was about to tell her. I don't know everything that happened before she saw me, but she seemed upset. Her harsh response has stuck with me all my life.

"Don't even come to me. Go in there, sit on that pot, and let it out right now," she yelled. "You need to learn how to keep things out of your mouth."

When I think about Grandma Nora's response, I can still picture her standing with her hands on her hips and hear the frustration in her voice. I now believe she was more upset with our parents having so many children than my swallowing a penny.

I must have been about four years old. We already had five or six girls in the family. We were like stair steps—about a year apart in ages. I can imagine what Grandma thought.

All these babies 'bout to drive me crazy. Every time I look up, somethin' done happen to one of 'em. Annie Mae and Herbert

3

are just too young to be having all them children. I don't see how they gonna take care of 'em. Every year they have another one. And they don't seem to be able to have nothing but girls. Herbert needs to have some boys to help him on that farm.

My feelings were crushed. I remember leaving the room that day, but I don't know what happened to the penny. I don't recall seeing it again, having any difficulties, or my parents mentioning it.

That was the only time I remember seeing my grandparents. My parents told us both of them passed when we were young. I imagine we visited them often because we lived on a nearby farm.

That day was my earliest memory of what would be a family of nine girls growing up on farms in Virginia. It was also my first realization of being involved in a journey that would involve my family's moving from one farm to another. For young parents trying to rear a large family during the late 30s through the 60s, times were tough with years of struggle. In spite of all of the hardships, our family experienced joy and triumphs.

Herbert Lee Harris and Annie Mae DeLoatch, our parents, met when they were young. Their families lived in Southeastern Virginia.

Mama, the second daughter of Reddick and Queen Esther Deloatch, was born May 28, 1920 in Isle of Wight County. She had two sisters, St. Clara and Rosa. She also had three brothers, Ollie, James, and Edward. Her father lost his life from injuries that he received when he fell off a boxcar as he worked for the railroad. Sometime after his death, the family moved to Southampton County and settled in the farming community of Unity.

Born in Southampton County October 20, 1917, Daddy was the youngest son of Eddie and Nora Whitney Harris. He had one sister, Ora, and one brother, Charlie. They also lived on a farm in Unity.

As young children, our parents attended school together. When they were in their teens, they married. Daddy was 18 and Mama was just 15. Shortly thereafter, they began to increase their family. Their first child, a boy, was born in 1936. He lived only a few days after birth. Every one to two years for the next twenty years, another child was born. All girls. Ten girls. The last girl, born in 1953, passed shortly after birth, which left the family with nine girls.

We never knew when Mama was expecting another child except for the last sister. They didn't talk about having a baby, and friends didn't give baby showers. Early the next morning after a new baby was born, we heard cries, and one of our parents said, "Y'all come and see your new sister."

The first sister I remember seeing shortly after birth was Ernell. Her skin was quite red, and she was crying as most newborns do.

All of us, except the last girl, were born at home with the assistance of Cousin Sarah or Cousin Lou, midwives from nearby communities. Sometime during the night, they came and assisted Mama with the birth of the babies. Of course, we thought they brought the babies with them.

We never heard Daddy leave to get the ladies and didn't hear the babies crying or any other sounds to indicate a child was being born until the morning after. The midwife was gone by that time. Gone after another girl was added to the family.

With Mama's last pregnancy, some of us were in our teens and knew she was having another baby. I don't remember being told, but somehow we knew. The pregnancy was difficult. Mama became ill, was hospitalized, and gave birth in the hospital.

All of us were born near the small town of Zuni and the Black Creek community—farming areas in the southeastern part of Southampton County, one of Virginia's largest counties.

Historically, Southampton County is where the Nat Turner Rebellion, also known as the Southampton Insurrection, took place in 1831. The uprising, led by Turner, a slave, attempted to free Negro slaves in the South. Many Whites were killed, but the rebellion ended after a few days.

A religious man, Turner had many visions, which he believed were spirits guiding him. After witnessing a solar eclipse on February 12,1831, he became convinced that it had been a sign from God and began preparing for the rebellion. On August 12, 1831 the sun's bluish-green appearance was believed to be the final signal. A week later, he and more than 70 men began the rebellion.

After the rebellion, many slaves thought to have been part of the uprising were executed. Across the South, state legislatures passed laws prohibiting the education of slaves and restricting rights of assembly and other civil rights of free Negroes.

Nat Turner survived by hiding for several months. He was eventually captured, tried, convicted, and hanged.

Except for that bit of history, the county is probably not noted for much more than its small farms with rich soil where corn, cotton, peanuts, and soybeans have been grown as long as I can remember. Although the area where our family's journey began long ago has changed with the times, some parts are pretty much like they were during our childhood. We look forward to visiting the county and have many memories of the people and events that impacted our lives and made us who we became.

How We Got Our Names

Then the people began to multiply on earth,
and daughters were born to them.
Genesis 6:1

Being young and having to choose appropriate names for us was probably not an easy task for Mama. So, our relatives and some of the older white ladies in the community assisted in the selection of our names. Mama had ideas about how she wanted to name us but probably compromised far too often. The older ladies undoubtedly had good intentions, but some of us were given names that caused a lot of grief and ridicule.

Most of us had nicknames, probably used because of difficulty in pronouncing our given names. It's not clear why others were chosen.

The first child, Herbert Lee Harris Jr., named after our father, lived only a few days. I don't imagine our parents ever dreamed the rest of their children would all be girls.

Grandmother, Queen Esther, wanted the first girl to be named after her. For unknown reasons, she was named Queen Elizabeth. What a name—probably perfect for the Queen of England or some other royal, but not a name that boosted our sister's self- esteem. She hated it and was always teased about it. She dropped the name Queen after she left the county. Then the family called her Elizabeth.

Her nickname, Bootjack, was just as far-fetched. No one seems to know the exact reason why she was given that name. Only family members used the name, so it wasn't too much of a problem for her.

Ruby Mae and Rebie Mae were the second and third girls. Since Ruby was born in July, Mamma named her after the gemstone for that month. We called her Sissy.

Rebie was the name of Daddy's first cousin. Mama's middle name was Mae—a name that many people in the community used as middle names for their children. We had Edith Mae and Shirley Mae, along with cousins, Hazel Mae and Ora Mae. Ruby and Rebie had little trouble with their names. Many people just didn't know how to pronounce the name Rebie. She was sometimes called Rah Rah.

When I was born, the ladies in the community began to take an active role in naming us. It seems as though they assumed Mama would give birth to another girl, so she said they were anxious to name one of us.

I am the fourth girl and was named Daphne Louise by Esther Womble, the owner of the farm where we lived. As I grew older and could recognize my name in print, we found an old Greek Mythology book that Mrs. Womble left in the farmhouse. For a long time, I could only recognize the word Daphne in it. While looking through it, I tried to see how many times I could find my name. After learning to read, I discovered that the book was the story of Daphne and the Greek God, Apollo.

So that's where Mrs. Womble got my name. For years, I believed I was the only Daphne in the world. I met another girl with the same name when I was about eighteen years old.

The biggest problem with my name was in the schools and the community; no one knew how to pronounce and spell it, not even my teachers. When seeing my name for the first time, they always hesitated, and I had to say it for them. I was called Daphine, Dalphine, Daffadene, Dalphony, Daffy, and Dafhonie, just to list a few. Most of them continue to call me Daphine. One of the senior members of our church simply called me Daffodil. The family called me Dap.

Before graduating from high school, I was determined to set the record straight on the legal spelling of my name. I wanted so badly to have my name written correctly on my diploma that I went to the school secretary and requested to have corrections made.

"Please make sure that my name is written correctly," I insisted. "The correct spelling is D-A-P-H-N-E, not D-A-P-H-I-N-E." On graduation day, I proudly received my diploma awarded to Daphne Louise Harris.

Minnie Pearl was the fifth girl. She was the second to be named by the ladies in the community. Mrs. Rosa Powell and her sister Laura had the honor of naming her.

"Can we name her Minnie Virginia?" one of them asked.

No one seems to know why Minnie Pearl was the name selected other than it was the name of a popular country music singer at the Grand Ole Opry in Nashville, Tennessee at the time.

What a disaster! That name brought fame and notoriety to the renowned singer, but it was certainly not the best name for a young black girl growing up in Southampton County, Virginia at that time. I'm sure those ladies had no clue how much anguish Minnie would suffer because of it.

A walk through the halls at school drew taunts of "Minnie Pearl, Minnie Pearl, where are your pearls? Or "Minnie Pearl, Minnie Pearl, where's your straw hat?"

Minnie grew lean and tall, so the children also called her Skinny Minnie. The family called her Minnie or Minnie Poo.

"I hated to say my full name," Minnie recalled. "There were times when I had to state it, and people laughed at me. So, I unofficially dropped the name Pearl. I now sign my name Minnie P. Harris."

Years ago, it was evident that Minnie had put the name Pearl out of sight, but not completely out of mind. I imagine she had done whatever she could to make it work. Rather than continue to detest it, she felt it was okay to make light of it. At our family reunion as the nine of us introduced ourselves, Minnie stood with a wide straw hat on her head and hands on her hips.

Echoing the voice of the Grand Ole Opry star, she said loudly, "How-w-w dee-e-e. My name is Minnie Pearl. I'm just so proud to be here."

Her gesture received laughs from the group, and that was exactly what she expected.

The sixth girl, Ernell was named after Dr. Ernell Harris, the only African American medical doctor in the city of Franklin, Virginia at that time. Mama didn't rely on anyone to help her with that name. Ernell liked her name and had no problems with it. She accepted being named after someone well known in the area. When she was born, her complexion was quite red, so the family called her Red for many years.

When Eileen Beatrice, the seventh sister, was born, the ladies in the community named her. We don't remember which one had the honor and where she got the name, but it was just not one we were accustomed to hearing. It was also difficult for us to pronounce. So for many years, we called her Argie, short for Audrey, and the name Mama wanted to give her—one with which we were familiar. In school, she was called E-leen or Elaine. She never used her middle name.

No one seems to know how Yvonne, the eighth girl got her name. It was probably just a name that Mama liked. Yvonne liked her name but always said, "I wonder why I was not given a middle name. I guess Mama had just run out of middle names."

We sometimes called her Von or Evon.

When Ruth Ann, the ninth girl was born, we were attending church more often, and religion impacted our family. She was named after the book of Ruth in the Bible. We also lived near the Bowers' family who had given many of their children biblical names—Joseph, Mary, Isaac Paul, and Martha.

Ruth was sometimes called Rutabaga, a type of turnip grown in the area.

Annie, the tenth girl, who was named after our mother, lived only a few days after birth. Mama was hospitalized, so Daddy had a private burial for Annie.

It may sound cruel, but when Annie was born, we were not looking forward to having another girl in the family. We didn't like the responses we heard from grownups when Mama and Daddy told them they had nine children, all girls. We remember the old folks making comments like, "Annie Mae, is that another girl? How many churen you got now? Nine? All girls? No boys? You have all them girls and no boys? My, my, you got enough girls for a softball team. Lord, I know y'all wanted some boys, but you just have to take what God give you."

I remember Aunt Gertie said, "Lord, look at all them little chilluns," as we walked out on the porch to greet her when she came to visit us one day.

We were tired of hearing such comments. Having another sister meant there would be ten girls. What remarks will people make then? Will they say something else that will embarrass us?

We didn't want any more sisters. As far as we were concerned, nine girls in the family were enough. We would have been happy to have brothers, but no more sisters.

THE WOMBLE FARM

I know all the things you do. I have seen your hard work
and your patient endurance.
Revelation 2:2

Like his father, Daddy was a farmer. The family lived on several farms—the Ritter Place, Jim Field Place, the Womble Farm, the Beale Farm, and the Belkov Farm. Most of the farms had names associated with the landowners.

Daddy didn't own any of the farms. We were sharecroppers—an agreement that allowed tenants to live on farms and cultivate the land for a share of the profit from the crops produced. Landowners provided seed, fertilizer, and other supplies. They sometimes assisted with harvesting the crops.

Until I was in third grade, we moved from one farm to another. I remember two of them more than the others. The first one was the Womble Farm. Daddy had worked for George Hunter and Esther Womble for several years. Our family lived in a small two-room house at the edge of the farm. I was too young to know much about it, but was told I was born there.

Before I became old enough to go to school, the Wombles left their land and entrusted Daddy with the farming. That was an awesome responsibility. It was Daddy's first time being totally in charge of a farm. None of us were old enough to help him. He and Mama had to do the work. And there was much to be done.

Our family moved into the large farmhouse. Boy, did we need the extra room because the family was growing rapidly. The two-story house had four bedrooms, a kitchen and a dining room. We were allowed the use of only three bedrooms. The door to the fourth bedrooms was always locked. We peered through the skeleton keyhole but couldn't see anything except the bright sunlight shinning through the window.

"I can't let y'all go in that room," Mama said. "Miss Esther left some of her furniture in there. She'll be back to get it."

As long as we lived there, we never saw inside the room and didn't see Miss Esther come to get anything out of it. She visited us, but I can't remember her taking the furniture away with her. I still wonder what was really in there.

The house had plenty of room, but it didn't have electricity. Many homes in rural Southampton County did not have electric power in the forties. In fact, I was in third grade before we lived in a house with electricity. Kerosene lamps and lanterns were used for light.

Wood burning stoves, which were used to heat the house, were also used for cooking and heating water for bathing and washing clothes. Two large black cauldrons outside were filled with water. A fire was built around them to heat the water. Since there were so many of us, we were always in need of clean clothes and diapers.

Large tin tubs and washbasins were used for bathing. It was impossible to take a bath every night. Lots of what we called "wash-ups" were done, using small washbasins.

Tubs were also used for washing clothes. Laundry was done by hand using a washboard and put outside on clotheslines to dry. When there were periods of bad weather, it was difficult to always have enough clean clothes.

We had no indoor plumbing. Outhouses and chamber pots that we called "pee buckets" served as toilets. The pots had to be brought in at night, taken out each day, and emptied in the outhouse. We feared snakes and spiders that were sometimes lurking inside. All the old magazines, newspapers, and catalogs could be found there. The family couldn't afford to purchase toilet tissue.

Water was drawn from an open well with a bucket. The bucket was always falling in the well. Daddy got it out with a long pole that had a hook on the end. Once, I almost fell into the well while trying with all my might to keep the bucket from falling. I was probably six years old. As I climbed the side, Mama raced to the well to stop me. She kept screaming, "Daphne, Daphne, get down. Get down Daphne. Get down, now."

I kept climbing as I held onto the rope.

"The bucket ain't in the well," I yelled. The bucket ain't in the well."

Luckily, Mama got to me before I got over the rim of the well. By that time, I had retrieved the bucket.

"Don't you do that again," she said. "Never. Just stay away from the well. If you fall in there, you will drown."

I was determined to keep that bucket from falling but didn't have a clue of the danger involved. I don't remember climbing the side of the well again. That could have resulted in a more tragic experience than some of the misfortunes that we had as a family.

Just as most of the farmers, Daddy planted corn, peanuts, cotton, and soybeans. Two mules, Peter Jack and Mouse, and a mare named Gray Jack were used for tilling and plowing the fields. No one seems to know why Jack was a part of the names for the animals. Day after day, Daddy walked up and down the fields behind the animals with plows, cultivating the crops. He was an excellent farmer. He knew exactly what to do to make crops grow—the type of seeds to plant, the correct amount of fertilizer to use, and the right time to harvest.

Every year in early spring, he picked up a copy of *Farmer's Almanac* at the country store and used the phases of the moon and other information to guide him in planting crops. Corn was usually planted by May 15 and peanuts by June 1.

Using a stake, he could form rows that were as straight as arrows. When one was done, the others seemed to magically take shape, equal distances apart.

After a few years, Gray Jack died. Daddy attached a rope to her neck and dragged her to the open field. With the help of some of his friends, he dug a giant hole and buried her. That was a terrifying sight. I was so traumatized that for a long time I couldn't sleep at night. I sat very quietly and stared at the windows. I could visualize the lifeless carcass of Gray Jack in that huge hole. I know my parents had no idea how much the death of that horse affected me. They probably didn't realize that young children might do better if they aren't exposed to things of that nature at such an early age.

Other animals on the farm included a cow, which supplied milk for the family. Daddy milked it daily. He sat on a stool and collected the milk in a pail. Trying to teach us to perform that chore didn't work at all.

"Don't be scared," he said. "Squeeze it into the bucket."

Rebie recalled trying to learn to milk the cow.

"As soon as I got started, the cow kicked me in one direction and the bucket in another. After that, Daddy told me to go on to the house.

" 'I have to milk the cow myself', he said. 'I don't want the cow to hurt you or waste all the milk.'

"Daddy gave up trying to teach us after that incident."

We certainly needed the milk. We drank fresh milk after it was chilled in the icebox. With no electricity, we didn't have a refrigerator. We used an icebox instead. Large blocks of ice, purchased from the iceman or the country store, were put in the icebox to keep food cold. As the milk chilled, cream rose to the top of the containers, was skimmed, and used to make butter. Some of the milk was allowed to curdle and form what was called "clabber," which tasted like buttermilk.

Mama taught us how to make butter by churning the cream. It was fun to see butter as it became visible in the container after turning the handle on the churn around and around. She also taught us how to make butter by putting cream in a Mason jar and shaking it up and down on our laps.

"Now shake it. Keep shaking it until you see butter," she said.

After we shook the jar for what seemed like forever, and sang, "Come butter, come," the soft yellow butter appeared like magic.

"Now let's put it in this mold and put it in the icebox."

The wooden mold had the shape of a flower carved on it. That was imprinted on the butter when it hardened and was ready to eat. Freshly made butter with hot biscuits was always a treat.

Hogs were raised and sold to get money to support the family or slaughtered for pork products. Once a year, Hog Killing took place on the farm. Friends and neighbors helped Daddy butcher the hogs and prepare hams, sausage, and slabs of bacon to be cured in the smokehouse. The meat was covered with salt and left in the smokehouse for several days. Later, it was hung from the rafters, and smoldering wood was used to give it a smoked flavor.

Excess fat was cooked outside in a large black pot to extract oil from the meat. Most of the oil was allowed to harden and form lard, which was used for cooking just as vegetable oils are used today. A mixture of lard and lye was used to make soap, which was used mostly for cleaning the house and washing clothes.

The ladies usually had the job of preparing the sausage and chitterlings—intestines from the hog— or "chitlins" as the locals called them. First, they emptied the intestines of the feed and other partially digested matter that the hogs had eaten. Next, using a long rod, they turned them inside out. After turning, washing, and rinsing them several times, they were cooked and put in the icebox. What an awful odor. For days, everything in and around the house smelled like the innards of hogs.

Every spring, Mama ordered hundreds of baby chicks, which we called biddies. The postman delivered them in cardboard boxes with peepholes to ensure they got plenty of fresh air. Some of the chickens looked like little black balls of cotton, and others were yellow. As youngsters, we were excited when the shipment arrived. Mama let us hold and feed some of them.

"Don't squeeze them and try not to drop them," she said. "The black chicks are Barred Rocks and Dominickers, and the yellow ones are Rhode Island Reds. When they are eight weeks old, we can have chicken for supper, and in six months the hens will lay eggs."

Some of the chickens were raised to provide food for the family. Others, along with the eggs they produced, were sold at the country stores. No chickens were spared. All of them were eventually eaten or sold. I remember Old Red, the rooster that ruled the barnyard and chicken coop for a long time. Day after day, he chased us and everything else that invaded his domain. Although one of his legs had been broken, he continued to guard his area ferociously. I remember waking up to his crowing each morning as the sun rose.

When Mama finally took Old Red to the chopping block and later cooked it for supper, some of us were reluctant to eat it. Nobody rushed to the table when Mama said, "Supper is ready. Y'all come and eat."

Minnie, who was about four years old, simply refused to come in the kitchen.

"Mm mm," she cried.

"What's wrong with you?" Mama asked.

"Mm mm," she continued to cry.

By that time, Mama was really annoyed.

"What is the matter with you? Don't you want something to eat?"

"Yeah. But uh, uh, I, I don't want, I don't want none of that old shicken," Minnie said.

Because the rooster was so mean and aggressive, Minnie was afraid to eat it. Needless to say, she settled for biscuits and whatever vegetables we had that evening. For a long time, she didn't like chicken.

Large domesticated white geese were also kept on the farm. They were eaten, and their down was used to stuff pillows. The geese were protective of their young goslings and didn't hesitate to react if we got too close to them. Sometimes they attacked us. The welts we got caused us indescribable pain.

"Don't be fooled into thinking that you can run away from the geese. They will fly to protect their young. So, stay away from them," Daddy warned.

Just as hogs, chickens, and geese provided food for the family, many fruit and nut trees, which had been planted, also added to our food supply. The apple, pear, damson, fig, peach, pecan, and black walnut trees made fresh fruit and nuts available for canning or eating.

We loved pecans and couldn't wait until late fall when the nuts fell from the huge trees that towered over the farmhouse. We had an uncanny habit of listening as the nuts fell on the tin roof of the house, then scurrying outside to be the first to find them as they rolled to the ground.

The fig tree was the only tree that was off-limits to us. I have vivid memories of it and where it grew, but the figs were forbidden fruit. For a long time, I didn't know why.

"Miss Esther wanted the figs," Ruby reminded me. "She usually came and picked them as they ripened."

We also had grapes that Mama used to make preserves. She sometimes used them to make wine, which was shared with relatives and friends.

We were forever climbing the trees or grape arbors to get fresh fruit. Sometimes after getting in the trees, we discovered that we weren't alone up there. Once Rebie and I climbed the pear tree and were planning to shake pears from it. As soon as we began to shake the branches, we spotted a huge black snake. The snake appeared to be just as startled as we were. It fell out of the tree and quickly slithered away. Rebie and I tumbled out of the tree and tried to run. I could barely move.

"My leg must be broke. I can't get up," I cried, while trying to stand. "I can't walk."

Rebie comforted me and tried to make me feel better. When I was finally able to stand, she kept saying, "You don't hurt that bad, do you? You don't hurt that bad, do you?"

I guess she knew she was in big trouble because she was older, and it was probably her idea to go to the pear tree anyway. I simply followed her as I did quite often.

I managed to hobble to the house. We were afraid to tell Mama and decided not to say anything. Trying to act as though nothing happened didn't work. She found out about our mishap. My limping let her know that I was in pain.

"What's wrong with you?" Mama asked.

"We were in the pear tree trying to get pears and saw a snake."

"And you fell out of the tree, didn't you?"

"Yeah, both of us."

"I told y'all to stay out of that tree. Wait until the pears fall off the tree if you can't reach them."

Sometimes long poles could be used to knock fruit from the trees. That day we thought it would be easier to climb the tree. Instead of fruit, we got bumps and bruises.

My back and leg hurt for a few days. I really didn't get injured badly, and we weren't punished. I still have a mental picture of the snake and our falling. I don't remember climbing that tree again as long as we lived on the Womble Farm. If we couldn't reach the pears or our parents couldn't get them for us, we learned to wait until some fell to the ground.

We enjoyed the outdoors. When we weren't climbing trees, we liked walking along the road and fields or into the woods to gather blackberries, blueberries, wild grapes, or whatever we could find. We knew every trail or path nearby. We learned to watch out for snakes, poison ivy, briers, and other thorny plants. We had so many areas to explore and no boundaries as long as we didn't stray from the farm.

ROSENWALD SCHOOL

If your gift is serving others, serve them well.
If you are a teacher, teach well.
Romans 12:7

While living on the Womble Farm, we attended Rosenwald School. I was six years old when I was enrolled in first grade. Daddy took us the first day. Mama had to stay at home and take care of our younger sisters.

The county didn't have kindergarten in the public schools. At least, that was the case in schools for Negro children. The school district was racially segregated. White children attended consolidated schools while Negro children attended several small schools located throughout the county. We weren't aware of all the opportunities offered in the racially divided schools.

Elizabeth, Ruby, and Rebie were already in school, and I was excited to go with them. Miss Whitney, Daddy's first cousin whom he called Gladys, taught grades 4-7, and Mrs. Ross, my first teacher, taught grades 1-3.

"Elizabeth and Ruby will be in Gladys's room," Mama said.

She didn't tell us that the children wouldn't call the teacher Gladys. So, when she said, "Hello boys and girls, my name is Miss Whitney," Elizabeth thought Mama had made a mistake.

"I thought your name was Gladys," she said.

"It is, but you will have to call me Miss Whitney."

So, at school, we called her Miss Whitney. When not at school, we said, "Cousin Gladys."

We lived about three miles from school and walked each day. Frank Clark, a farmer who lived nearby, allowed us to take a short cut through his pasture. That made the distance about a mile. I still have vivid memories of the green grass in the spring and the animals grazing as we walked through the field. I also remember the clumsy baby calves trying to keep up with the rest of the herd. I was afraid of the cattle, especially the bulls, and often said," Let's be quiet and walk fast so they won't see us."

No matter how quietly we walked, the cattle seemed to sense we were nearby. We could see their large eyes as they stopped grazing and looked our way. Sometimes they mooed and caused the cowbells around their necks to ring. We had to be careful in order to avoid stepping in the awful smelling piles of cow manure, scattered throughout the area. Had we stepped in some of that stuff and carried it to school on the soles of our shoes, our names would have been mud or some other name I don't want to say.

With our noses pinched, we went "phew" each time we passed the large brown lumps. As soon as we got through Mr. Clark's pasture, we could see the school. The old unpainted wooden building was built so high above ground that we sometimes played in the crawl space beneath it. By the end of recess, we were quite dusty and dirty. The playground was bare. Not even a seesaw or swing was provided.

The rural school was said to be one of 5,000 schools established for Negro children in the 1900s by Julius Rosenwald. The project was a major effort to improve the quality of public education for African Americans in the South in the early twentieth century.

The school had two large rooms, one for grades 1-3, and the other housed grades 4-7. The huge windows had shades that were always raised in the morning and lowered to the same level in the afternoon. We enjoyed drawing or coloring pictures to decorate the windowpanes during the year. We were eager to see the drawings our teacher chose to display. There were shouts of "I see mine." "I see mine." "Do you see yours?" In spring, we made tulips and other flowers. During the fall months, the windows were usually decorated with colorful leaves or turkeys for Thanksgiving. We could expect to see trees with bells for Christmas and snowmen for the winter months.

Each room had a black pot-bellied stove that kept us warm and cozy in winter. Many years later, I learned that someone from the community came early each morning and made fires before school began.

Two blackboards were mounted across the front of the room. It was exciting to write on them or complete math exercises. It was also fun just to be able to erase and wash them at the end of the day.

Cloakrooms were provided for our coats and lunch pails. A pump in that area was where we could get water.

Two outhouses, one for girls and one for boys, were located near the woods.

We sometimes saw spiders, lizards, snakes, and wasps near them. Just like at home, I didn't want to use them because of the animals and insects. I was also afraid of falling into that deep dark hole over which they were built. I usually waited each day until I got home or to the wooded area near Mr. Clark's farm.

Although the educational level of our parents was limited, they tried to help us as much as they could. Daddy completed seventh grade, and Mama left school at the end of sixth grade. They practiced reading, handwriting, and spelling assignments with us. They also assisted with math.

Like most parents, they taught us to recite and sing the alphabet and write our names before going to school. The names were not always written correctly, using the method our teachers used. I remember my teacher giving me a practice sheet showing how my name should be written.

"Write your name just like this," she said, pointing to the letters.

Of course, for a long time, I formed my letters just as Mama had taught me. With a little practice, I learned to form the letters as my teacher had instructed.

Mama taught us nursery rhymes she learned in school. She also told stories she heard as a child. We just loved hearing her tell the Uncle Remus story about Br'er Rabbit's begging not to be thrown into the briar patch as he tricked his captor.

"And Br'er Rabbit pleaded, 'Please, please don't throw me in the briar patch. Please, please don't throw me in the briar patch,'" Mama said.

We also enjoyed listening to Uncle Remus stories on the radio after school.

I don't remember much about my first year of school except learning, reading, writing, and arithmetic. Reading was taught with books about Dick, Jane, and their dog Spot. We also learned to read from books about a curious little monkey named Winky, who wore a red cap.

"Oh yes, I remember reading sentences like 'Run, run. See Winky run' when I was in first grade," Minnie recalled.

During that time, families had to purchase textbooks for their children. Books were taken home each day. Mrs. Ross assigned pages that she wanted us to know how to read in our books the next day.

"Get your mama and daddy to help you practice reading in your book each night," she said.

For homework, we read each page over and over every night until we finished all the books for the grade level. If students were smart and completed all the books for their grade level, could write well, and do well in arithmetic, sometimes they were skipped to the next grade. None of us skipped a grade.

We enjoyed going to school, and Rebie and I liked Mrs. Ross. Just as most children, we wanted to do well and wanted our teachers to like us. Sometimes we took them things from the farm. We couldn't do the apple for my teacher treat because the apples on the farm weren't always the best quality. We could take pecans, peanuts, or sometimes grapes—so we thought. After taking a Mason jar of grapes to our teacher one year, we realized that was a no-no. Being young children, we thought freshly picked scuppernong grapes would be the perfect treat. All went well. We were graciously thanked and thought the gesture was really appreciated.

Many days later, we played Hide and Seek in the crawl space beneath the school during recess. What we found really surprised us. We discovered our jar still filled with grapes.

The strangest feeling came over me. I couldn't believe what I saw. Even today, I have vivid memories of finding the jar. I still can't understand why our teacher didn't take the treats home and spare us our hurt feelings. What we thought were the ripest and most delicious grapes had been picked from the arbor. We thought she would surely like them.

We didn't dare tell the other children. We were afraid if we told them, they would remember the jar of grapes we had given to our teacher and tease us about it. Our teacher wasn't told, but we couldn't wait to get home and tell Mama what we saw.

"Mama, Mama! We were playing under the school today and saw the jar of grapes that we gave our teacher," Rebie said, as we got home from school that day.

"Under the school," Mama asked? "You saw what?"

"We saw the jar full of grapes that we gave to our teacher. She must have thrown them under the school," I said. "Wonder why did she do that?"

"I don't know," Mama said, shaking her head from side to side. "I don't know."

"Did you tell her what you saw?"

"No, we didn't tell her. We were too scared to say anything. We just left the jar where we saw it."

"That's okay," Mama said. "I just don't understand. I know one thing, I will never let y'all take anything else to that teacher."

Sometimes, Mama sent notes to our teacher when matters needed to be discussed. I don't know how our parents handled that situation. I know we never took anything else to school for Mrs. Ross. In fact, I don't remember our taking anything else to any of our teachers.

In December of that year, our family moved to another farm, and we were transferred to a new school. Finding the jar under the school made us feel sad and dislike our teacher. We were happy to no longer attend that school.

It's An Emergency

Cry for help, but will anyone answer you?
Job 5:1

Like most families, we had our share of emergencies and near tragic experiences as young children. Our home was not child proofed, so accidents were waiting to happen. It was probably a miracle that more unpleasant things didn't occur. Getting assistance was difficult since emergency services were not readily available in the county, and the family didn't have access to telephones during that time.

The most frightening mishap for me personally was the day that I swallowed a small open safety pin as I sat holding one of my younger sisters. As I leaned back with my mouth opened, she dropped the pin into it. I sat up rather than try to spit it out. I realized that the pin was in too far and could feel it scratching my throat as I swallowed it. I felt like I was swallowing a fish bone. I was so afraid that I screamed for Mama and Daddy. I'm not sure where they were at the time. Unlike the day I swallowed a penny and was taken to my grandparents' house, Mama said, "We have to take this child to see a doctor."

Off we went to see Dr. Babb, who had an office in Ivor. I don't remember much that happened at the doctor's office except being afraid and having the doctor ask me, "Can you feel the pin? Does it hurt?"

As most children, I was terrified of getting a shot. I wasn't in pain, and I don't imagine doctors in small rural areas had equipment to do X-rays. So, there was no way of knowing where the pin was lodged in my body.

"Let her eat lots of bread and check her stool each day," the doctor said.

On the way home, Daddy stopped at the country store and purchased bread. He gave me the whole loaf.

"Eat that bread like the doctor said," Mama told me.

I ate until I could eat no more. We never saw the pin again. I never went back to see the doctor. Until this day, we don't know what happened to the pin. I often wonder if it might still be in my body.

That was the only time that I remember being taken to see a doctor as a child. Family members got no medical care unless they were very sick, needed shots, or had some type of injury. That was probably the case for most of the families in the area.

When preparing fields for planting in the early spring, farmers often used controlled burning to clear the areas of grass, weeds, and the remains of previous crops. That process made it easier to plow the fields before planting. It wasn't always a safe and easy task because farmers never knew when the wind would increase and cause the fires to burn out of control.

That's exactly what happened the day on the Womble farm when Daddy tried to clear a cornfield. The velocity of the wind changed, and the fire not only burned the field, but cinders set fire to the roof of the barn, as well as the woods nearby. No other house was in sight—no telephone to call for help and no fire department to respond.

Most farmers had large bells installed at the top of tall poles. With a long rope attached, they were normally sounded at noon to let workers know it was lunchtime. They were also tolled for emergencies

Luckily, we had a bell, which Daddy rang as loudly as he could and yelled, "Fire, fire! Help! Help!

As soon as the farmers nearby heard the bell and his cries for help, they rushed over. They could also see the black smoke billowing up. They knew in times like that, they had to band together and act quickly. One fire could destroy the entire community.

Unlike most structures on the farm, which had tin roofs, one small barn had a roof made of wooden shingles. It was about to be destroyed.

"Herbert, what you trying to do? How did the fire get started?" one farmer asked, rushing to put it out.

"I was just trying to burn some of the cornstalks and weeds to make it easy to plow this field."

Daddy quickly climbed on the roof of the barn and ripped off the burning shingles with a pickaxe. Using water, sand, shovels, and branches from the pine trees, the neighbors extinguished the flames in the woods. Luckily, not much of the forest was burning. With a plow, Daddy created a barrier around the field to contain the fire and keep it from continuing to spread.

The quick action of the neighbors prevented what could have been a real disaster for the family, as well as the community. Had the farmhouse caught fire and burned, I can't imagine where we would have lived. By that time, eight girls were in the family.

The day Ernell got burned was by far the mishap that affected our family most. As she and Minnie stood in front of the opening of our tin wood-burning stove, they were fascinated by the way their nightgowns could be drawn into the stove by the draft. Ernell's gown caught fire. It was winter with about three inches of snow on the ground. We were left in the house while our parents were doing chores.

As Ernell, who was almost four years old, ran around screaming with her gown in flames, we didn't know what to do. Some of us screamed for our parents while others stood stunned. "Stop, Drop and Roll," fire safety techniques, were not taught during fire drills in the schools at that time, and our parents had not taught us safety rules or warned us about the danger of getting too close to the stoves.

When Mama and Daddy heard our screams, they rushed to the house. With her gown in flames, Ernell ran out on the back porch where clothes were soaking in a tub of water. During that time, it wasn't uncommon for clothes to be soaked prior to being washed. Somehow, Ruby had the insight to grab some of the wet clothes and douse the flames.

Ernell was rushed to Raiford's Memorial Hospital in Franklin, where she stayed for days. She had suffered third-degree burns over a large portion of her body and was in critical condition. I didn't think we were ever going to see her again.

Mama and Daddy stayed at the hospital many nights. We were too young to be left at home alone, so we went to live with relatives. For most of us, it was the first time we had spent the night away from home without our parents. Uncle Charlie and Aunt Roberta Vick, who lived in Franklin, took one of my sisters and me to live with them. The rest of the girls went to live with other relatives in the area. We missed many days of school.

Uncle Charlie tried to comfort us and make our stay a learning experience. Pointing to the clock one day, he asked, "What time is it?"

When no one answered, and he realized we were having difficulty, he said, "Y'all don't know how to tell time? Well, I think I can help you learn."

Moving the hands on the clock, he made statements like, "When the short hand is on eight and the long hand is on twelve, it's eight o'clock." "Now, what time is it?"

"Eight o'clock."

"What time is it now?"

"Nine o'clock."

He drilled us daily after getting home from work. When it was time for us to go home, we knew how to tell time at least to the hour and half hour.

After we went home, Mama and Daddy continued to spend most of their time at the hospital. Grandma stayed at our house and took care of us. Ernell's condition was so serious that she had to be transferred to St. Phillip's Hospital in Richmond, VA, where she stayed for a long time. Specialized care and treatments, which included blood transfusions and skin grafts, were needed. The local hospital in Franklin couldn't perform those procedures.

Many days passed as our parents took trips to Richmond on weekends. Grandma continued to take care of us. Spring came and Ernell was still hospitalized. Shortly before Easter, as they got ready for the trip, Mama announced, "Ernell will be coming home soon. We'll bring her home when we go to see her on Sunday."

We were so happy and could hardly wait to see her. It seemed like she had been gone for a year although it had been only about four months. When she got home, she sang Easter songs. I remember her singing, "Here Comes Peter Cottontail" and other songs that the hospital staff had taught her. We learned to sing along with her.

I have vivid memories of the Easter basket she brought home. The chocolate bunny, jellybeans of many colors, and other treats were shared with all of us.

Unfortunately, our excitement about Ernell's being home didn't last long. It was difficult for Mama to control her. It took time for her to adjust to being home, and I imagine she missed all the attention she received from the hospital staff. For a long time, she wanted to have things her way. She was five years old by that time and wasn't like the little sister we had prior to her getting burned. The outbursts and temper tantrums were awful. We heard cries of, "Mama, Ernell hit me. Tell her to stop."

We couldn't push her away because she still had areas on her body that hadn't completely healed. I really think she sensed that we were at a disadvantage and took advantage of the situation. Mama just threw up her hands and said, "The nurses and doctors at that hospital really spoiled my child. When they gave her those transfusions, it must have been some bad blood."

About a year later, Ernell had to return to Richmond for a short period of time. A muscle in her leg prevented her from walking erectly. Corrective surgery to make walking more normal had to be done prior to her going to school. The surgery was successful, and she recovered nicely but will always have scars, which resulted from that awful day—the most tragic experience the family had to endure when we were young.

THE BEALE FARM

And he will send showers of rain
so every field becomes a lush pasture.
Zechariah 10:1

In December 1949 after school closed for Christmas break, like nomads we moved from the Womble farm to the Beale farm. All of our meager belongings were packed for the trip. I don't remember how everything was taken to the new place, which was about ten miles away. During that time, many farmers didn't have trucks. It wasn't uncommon to see them with their belongings loaded onto large horse-drawn wagons or carts as they moved from one farm to another. I imagine that's what happened in our case.

For the first time, we would live in a house with electricity. We were so excited to see the new place.

"All you have to do is put a light bulb in a socket, pull a cord, and you'll have light," Daddy said.

We wouldn't have to deal with those oil lamps with globes that always had soot on them, which had to be cleaned so more light could shine through. Also, we feared the wick in the lamp would burn down too far and cause the kerosene to explode.

Many things were different on the new farm. We had only one barn. Attached to it were stables for the cow and two mules, Mouse and Peter Jack. A chicken coop, all fenced in with chicken wire, an outhouse, and a smoke house were located in the yard behind the farmhouse.

Unlike the house on the Womble farm, which had plenty of room, the new farmhouse was really small—only three large rooms. In the middle of the ceiling of each room was a receptacle with a bare light bulb and a cord in it, waiting to be pulled, just as Daddy had told us.

"This house is just too little," Mama complained. "There's not enough room for all of us. Where will everybody sleep? There's not even enough space for the beds."

It certainly didn't have enough room for a family of ten. By that time, Yvonne had been born.

Until two rooms were added, our family lived in those three rooms. One room was used as the kitchen and the other two as bedrooms. Mama and Daddy slept in one room. A large hall could also be used for sleeping, but the eight of us girls slept in the same room. We had two single beds and one double. Somehow all of the beds were put in that room. One or two girls slept at the head and foot of each bed. Someone was always saying, "She's taking all of the blanket, get your feet off me, stop kicking me, or I'm about to fall off the bed."

None of the rooms had closets. We shared one chest. Each sister had a drawer or section for personal items. We had to learn to share and respect each other's space. As most siblings, we argued about each other taking too much space in the drawers. Some of us stored our belongings in cardboard boxes under the beds. We also quarreled about each other's not doing her share of the chores. We became skillful at cleaning one side of the room or making one side of the bed.

"Something's got to be done quickly to make more room for us," Mama said.

The landowner had promised to add more rooms. Months later, the addition of a kitchen and dining room was begun. That would allow us to have extra bedrooms.

Day after day, we watched the rooms being built. We collected all of the scrap pieces of building materials to use for making playhouses, kites, sleds, and other things. Hammers, nails, and handsaws were available, and we were allowed to handle them. Sometimes we injured our fingers, but not seriously.

As soon as the addition was completed, Mama changed her mind. "I want to use the extra space as a living room," she said. "We need a place to sit when company comes."

With that, our sleeping arrangements didn't change right away. A sleep sofa, chairs, and tables were purchased. As we got older and after Ruth, the ninth girl, was born, some of us slept in the living room. During the summer and early fall, when it wasn't cold, some of us slept on a bed in the hallway.

A piano was also purchased. Our parents wanted us to learn to play it, but we had no money for lessons. After looking at an ad in a magazine, Mama purchased home study books from the United States School of Music and hoped we could learn to play that way. Most of us learned a few tunes. Elizabeth seems to have benefitted from the program more than the rest. She learned how to play several songs fairly well.

Having a new kitchen and dining room enabled us to have room for a refrigerator, freezer, and wringer washing machine. We no longer had to go to town for ice, and it was much easier to wash our clothes. We still had no indoor plumbing—running water as we referred to it. We had to draw water from a pump in the middle of the yard. A bucket with water was kept nearby for use in starting the flow of water in the pump, especially when the water level was low. We called that "priming the pump." In the cold winter, the water in the pump sometimes froze, and a small fire had to be set around it to thaw the water.

Daddy planted a huge garden, which included tomatoes, peas, butter beans, corn, kale, collards, and cabbage. Sweet potatoes, cucumbers, beets, onions, and white potatoes were also planted. Mama took classes offered by the county on canning or freezing meats, fruits, and vegetables. Whatever Daddy planted or raised was canned or put in the freezer.

Mama took pride in preserving food for the family. She usually had a well-stocked freezer of meats and lots of Mason jars filled with fruits and vegetables, which provided food most of the year. With little space to store all of the canned goods, Mama stored them neatly under her bed.

Being such a large family, we sometimes ran out of food, especially during the winter months. Because of that, most of us learned what it means and how it feels to be hungry.

Missing from the Beale farm were the fruit and nut trees and grape arbors. We sometimes got pears from a tree in the yard by a vacant house down the road from us. Other fruits were purchased from farmers nearby. Mama made lots of preserves.

"In school, our lunch was biscuits and preserves most of the time," Minnie recalled. "We took biscuits and preserves to school so much that when we opened our little brown bags, the children laughed and said, 'biscuits and preserves.'" Having no grapes for wine didn't deter Mama. "I can still make wine," she said. "I will just use tomatoes and watermelon."

By that time, fields of watermelons and cantaloupes were planted. That venture didn't last long. Not much profit could be made from selling melons. I remember Daddy selling truckloads for five to ten cents per melon.

"For that amount of money, it's not worth it to keep planting melons," he said. "The folks at the markets don't want to pay anything for them."

Mama loved flowers. On one side of the yard, she had the most beautiful gladiolas, dahlias, zinnias, marigolds, petunias, and roses. In the front yard, she grew four-o'clocks, daffodils, and daylilies. Relatives and friends were always giving her plants. She had a green thumb for making them grow.

Having electricity meant that Mama could purchase a fancy new electric sewing machine and not have to use the old treadle one. Since money wasn't always available, she made many of our clothes after ordering fabric from Sears Roebuck, Spiegel, Aldens, and Montgomery Ward catalogs. When she couldn't get fabric, she used sackcloth. Feed for the animals, especially the chickens, was packed in thick cotton sacks, which had colorful designs and were called sackcloth.

Once when Mama was in such a hurry to sew something, she stitched right over one of her fingers, and part of the sewing machine needle broke off in it. Now, that was an emergency, but Mama didn't even seek medical help. She was quite a risk taker. I looked at her swollen finger as she soaked it in alcohol or liniment and wondered if it would get better. I wished she would see a doctor. We were so afraid, but she assured us that she would be just fine. A day or two later, she pulled the needle out of her finger, and it healed without complications.

Electric radios improved communication for the family. They were much easier to operate than the battery powered ones we had used before. It was important to be able to listen to reports, which broadcast the news, school closings, and weather. We also enjoyed listening to music. For a long time, we could only hear music played by Black recording artists late at night. Radio signals from Randy Records on WLAC-AM in Nashville, TN reached many states and transmitted rhythm and blues music in the 1950s.

Daddy was able to listen to the commodities and livestock reports of current prices for farm products. It was important for him to know how much to expect to be paid for hogs, eggs, corn, cotton, and most of what was produced on the farm when he took those goods to the market. He could also get that information from the newspaper.

Although the house was small, we had much more farmland than the acreage on the Womble farm. I imagine that was the reason Daddy moved from that farm. With children continuing to be born, he needed more land to produce products to sell to support the family.

Daddy needed help. As we got older and some of us were in our teens, we were required to do whatever needed to be done on the farm. Since there were no males in the family, we had to do chores that young boys usually performed. You name it. We did it.

With more land to cultivate, Daddy discussed buying a tractor.

"I don't want to keep using mules," he said. "It takes too long to get work done, and it's too much walking. I'll walk myself to death if I keep farming with mules."

Days later, a small tractor with detachable plows was delivered. Daddy had used the horse and mules so long that it took time for him to make the transition. He had to remember he couldn't use the same commands he used with the animals to operate the tractor. Several times, he came close to having accidents after saying "whoa, whoa" before realizing when he was using the tractor, he was no longer farming with mules and had to use the brake to stop the tractor.

Daddy continued to use the mules for many chores until they died. I don't remember Peter Jack's death. Mouse collapsed and died after wandering far into the woods one day.

More corn, cotton, and peanuts were planted. Weeds and grass had to be removed from the rows to ensure that the plants produced a bountiful harvest. We spent many days chopping and pulling weeds and grass. Farmers had not begun to use herbicides. We got hot and tired. Perspiration ran down our faces. At the end of each row, we spent time in the shade trying to get cool. Sometimes we dug holes in the soil to cool our hot feet. Leaves from poplar trees were placed under our straw hats to help cool our heads.

When Daddy didn't need us to work in the fields during the summer, we helped other farmers. Some of them paid us more than minimum wage, which was 75 cents an hour at that time. We worked for one dollar an hour. We really didn't mind doing that because it enabled us to have money for clothes and school supplies. Some of the money helped support the family. We also used the money to order fabric to make some of our clothes. We had learned to sew while watching Mama all those years.

During late summer and early fall, corn, cotton, and peanuts, had to be harvested. Corn was gathered by hand and stored in the barn. It was used to feed the animals or sold to get money to support the family. In our early years, Daddy took some of it to the local mill to be ground into corn meal to make bread.

Of all the chores that were done on the farm, we hated picking cotton most. It was picked and packed in large burlap bags that sometimes weighed more than 100 pounds. Bending for long periods of time with bags attached to our waists was hard work. Many times before taking the bags of cotton to the market, green cotton bolls were put in the sacks to make them weigh more.

Ruby recalled her experiences while in the cotton fields.

"Bags of cotton that I pulled one day were so heavy that I injured muscles in parts of my body. I was in so much pain I had to see a doctor.

"Our fingers got scratched when trying to get the cotton out of the bolls. Having scratched cuticles was painful and not attractive for young girls.

"Large green caterpillars with horns sometimes fed on the plants. They grew to what looked like three inches long. Their large droppings let us know if they were on the plants. The thought of just seeing one was terrifying. We were told that if bitten by one, we would die. I don't think that was true, but we were careful to avoid them. We didn't dare pick cotton from the plants until we located the pests and got rid of them. Thank God, there weren't many to contend with."

Sometimes Daddy hired someone to help with the cotton picking, so we wouldn't miss too many days of school. It was much easier to get the work done when others were there to talk to or sing along with. We also used transistor radios, which were available at that time, to listen to music while we worked.

Peanuts were the most profitable crop. The plants were dug and stacked on poles in the fields. After the plants dried for several weeks, a machine was used to separate the peanuts from the vines. That process was a dusty job. By the end of the day, the hairs in our nostrils looked like cobwebs, and we looked like we had been working in a coal mine. Most of the time, Daddy's friends helped with that chore. We missed school and helped when they were not available. The peanuts were put in large bags and sold to local grain dealers. The vines were left in the field or put in the hayloft to be used to feed the animals.

As years passed, many inventions made farming easier. Chemicals were used to kill weeds and grass. Advances were made in the development of corn, cotton, and peanut pickers. By the time the younger sisters got old enough to help on the farm, they didn't have much work. With all kinds of machinery, Daddy could do most of the work himself.

All of those experiences were enough to make us realize that we didn't want to live on farms when we grew up. We have the utmost respect and admiration for farmers and their crafts, but we paid our dues while growing up. Farming was done best by men and boys.

OUR OWN LITTLE WORLD

He will take delight in you with gladness.
With his love, he will calm your fears.
Zephaniah 3:17

The farms where we lived were isolated, and our experiences outside the home during our early years were quite limited. Only one house was in sight of the Womble farm, which was located along a dirt road. The Lewis family—Louise, Solomon, Jennie, Marie, and their mother lived there. That was the house where we lived before moving into the large farmhouse.

I couldn't stand Solomon. We were only seven years old, and he had decided that I was going to be his wife when we grew up. I didn't like that, not one bit. I enjoyed playing with his sisters but didn't like playing with him and hated going to school with him. Being teased about him by my sisters made matters worse. I always tried to think of mean words to say so that he wouldn't like me.

"Solomon thinks I love him, but I don't," I said. That was typical behavior for most young girls at that age. Since he and his sisters were the only children who lived near us, we had to play with them or live in complete isolation.

The Beale farm was more remote. It was a mile from the highway down a dirt road, which for a long time was not maintained by the county. We had no opportunities to sit on the front porch and watch traffic go by. It was like living in a world of our own. In winter, the road had so many holes that some of us named it Bumpy Hole Road. Getting the family car all the way to the house was sometimes impossible.

Two White families, the Scotts and the Bradshaws, lived across a field near us. The Scotts had two children, Johnny and Vivian. We never played with the children or even spoke to them. I always wondered where they went to school. They didn't walk with us, and I never saw them get on the yellow school bus that took the white children to school. The year their mother died after being ill for several days, we didn't know of her death until we saw cars drive slowly down the road on the day of her funeral.

The Bradshaws were elderly and their only son, Howard, who lived with them, appeared to be about Daddy's age. For a long time, we thought Howard would never find a wife. When he finally married, it was interesting to see him with his petite wife, who seemed to simply adore him. They sat so close to each other in his truck that it looked like only one person. After retiring, Howard and Daddy worked together part-time at a meatpacking plant. They had developed a friendship that lasted the rest of their lives.

All families shared the dirt road. The grownups communicated and were helpful when needed. That made it much easier for each family, especially when the holes in the road needed to be repaired or when vehicles got stuck in the mud.

The closest Black family, the Bowers, also lived along that road. Their house was close to the highway, which meant they lived almost a mile from us. All of their children had moved away except Joseph and Mary. Martha, their granddaughter, who was the same age as Ernell, lived there, also. It probably wasn't safe for Martha to walk to our house alone because of the wooded areas. We saw her at church and school. As she got older, she visited us on a sled pulled by her horse, Molly.

The Bowers were landowners although their farm was very small. They also had a telephone, which they let Daddy use to make important calls.

Other Black families, which included the Burts and the Whitfields, lived near us for short periods of time. I remember walking to school with the Burts but never visited them. Some of our younger sisters went to school with the Whitfields. Their brief stays didn't allow enough time for us to get to know either family well.

Being isolated when we were young made us fearful of many things. If we didn't recognize something and it moved or went "Boo," we were afraid of it.

"Most young children are afraid of the dark, but I was scared of the moon at night," Minnie recalled. "You couldn't get me to go outside at night when the moon was shining, especially during a full moon."

I was afraid of shooting stars. For some reason, I associated them with flying saucers and aliens from outer space. I certainly didn't stargaze at night.

The day on the Womble farm when we saw our first low-flying crop duster, we were in the yard playing as we heard the unusually loud roar of the aircraft in the distance. When it appeared over the horizon, we ran to the house as fast as we could. We had watched airplanes flying high in the sky, but that one was too close for comfort.

So, as the airplane got close, Elizabeth yelled, "Daddy, you better get your gun 'cause here comes Hitler. Here he comes, Daddy. Please don't let him get us."

It had been several years since Adolf Hitler committed suicide and World War II ended. Our parents continued to talk about the war. Being young children, we didn't fully understand what was happening. Daddy was our protector. As long as we had him and he had his gun, we felt safe.

Another day on the Beale farm, when we saw our first helicopter, we ran for our lives again. All we could see at first sight was the propeller twirling around.

"Look, that's a flying saucer," one of the younger girls screamed. The aircraft was probably descending as it approached the airfield in Franklin, which was five miles away. It was flying so low when we turned around to get a good look at it, we could see the pilot and passenger bent over laughing at us little bare-footed farm girls scurrying to the house.

Yvonne recalled being terrified of blimps. "They were huge and seemed to be moving so slowly I thought they were going to fall out of the sky. I don't remember being told anything specific about them or why they were often seen in the area, but whenever I saw one I ran in the house."

Minnie and Yvonne recalled a time when they had somehow developed a strange concept about people who drove Jeeps.

"Although we were in our early teens, we thought people who owned vehicles of that type were part of a roving band of gypsies who would rob and cast evil spells on us," Minnie explained. "So, the day we were home alone and two land surveyors, driving a Jeep, came to measure acreage of the farm, we hid in the nearby woods. We were so afraid that we followed paths through the woods to Mrs. Bowers' house, the neighbor who lived about a mile away. As we told her about our fears, she assured us that the men would not harm us."

"Those men are just measuring the land," Mrs. Bowers said. "They are not going to bother y'all and they are not gypsies. Y'all can stay here until your mama and daddy get home."

When Mama and Daddy got home, the house was empty. The men were about to leave, and our parents didn't know where we were.

"Did you see any children here," Daddy asked as the men got into their Jeep?

"We saw no children," one of them men said. "No one came to the door when we blew our horn."

In rural areas, it wasn't unusual for visitors to blow their horns rather than get out of their vehicles and knock on the door. Most families had dogs that barked, and the visitors didn't know how vicious they were.

"We knew when our parents were at home because they had to drive past the Bowers' house on the way," Yvonne said. "The minute we saw them pass, we hurried home and told them what had happened. They reassured us that the men wouldn't harm us. The next day, we had to contend with ticks and redbugs we had encountered during our walk through the woods."

Clouds of dust sometimes appeared along Bumpy Hole Road when people came to visit, especially Uncle James, Aunt Rebecca, and Cousin J. C., who lived in Franklin. Their car seemed to move so fast we thought it wouldn't stop. Uncle James always drove a pretty car and bought only Chryslers. His working for Camp Manufacturing Company, the lumber mill in Franklin, enabled him to buy new cars. Whenever he traded cars, the family came out to the farm to let us see them.

Once, I remember Daddy said, "Who's that coming, making all that dust? I bet that's James. I know he got a new car and is coming to show it to us."

Through the dust, we could see the chrome on the front end of the shiny new car.

"Yeah, I think that's him," Mama said.

By the time he got to the house and the dust settled, we were nowhere to be seen. We hid in another room or in the cornfields nearby because he was usually a little tipsy, and we were afraid of him.

Aunt Rebecca usually fussed about how fast he was driving and was upset by the time they got to our house.

"Where are the children?" Aunt Rebecca asked.

"They're here. They're just hiding," Mama said.

Aunt Rebecca continued to complain.

"I told James about driving fast like he got a race car. He's gonna scare those children to death. They won't ever get used to him."

Lack of exposure kept us in shells. It took a lot of coaxing, but eventually we came out and talked to them.

"Come here little girls," Uncle James said. "Let me see you." "What y'all hiding for?" "We're not going to hurt you."

Sometimes, after talking to us, he gave each of us a nickel or dime.

As we got older and they continued to visit, we learned not to fear our uncle. He was kind. I believe he loved all of us and never intended to frighten us. He and Aunt Rebecca took Rebie to live with them one summer.

Many of our relatives lived in the county, and we were accustomed to seeing them. They visited more often, and we saw them at church. We also saw our cousins at school.

Aunt Rosa, Uncle Edward, Uncle Charlie, and their families lived in surrounding communities. Uncle Charlie was a jovial, robust man who always greeted us with a smile on his face and a cigar in his mouth. I don't think he ever learned all our names. He simply gave us nicknames. He also had nine children—five girls and four boys.

Relatives who lived far away were amazed at how long it took to drive from the highway to our house. Many years after we had moved away and had the opportunity to attend a family gathering, Cousin Ernest talked about how he and his family came to visit us one night. He said jokingly, "That road was so bumpy, and they lived so far back in the woods, I thought we would never get there. We actually had to use a flashlight to help us find the house."

Cousin Ernest and his sister, Thelma, lived in Connecticut and were certainly not used to rural areas. When they visited, they were excited to see the animals and wanted to pet them. Our animals were not used to strangers. So, Daddy had to warn our cousins before letting them see the animals.

"Y'all can go to the pasture and look at the animals," Daddy said. "But, don't get too close to them. And don't try to ride the mare."

Uncle Aurelious, Daddy's half-brother, and his friend usually visited during the summer. Sometimes his daughters Courtnay, Agnes, Geraldine and Georgiana, and his son Aurelious came with him. The family lived in New Jersey. We were intrigued hearing them speak with New Jersey accents, which seemed more distinct and different to us at that time.

After Aunt Ora learned to drive and was able to own a car, she visited more frequently. She hated having to drive that bumpy road. Once her car was jarred so much as she drove through one of the holes that when she got to our house, she declared,

"Herbert, you got to do something about the holes in that road. I think I just lost my motor driving through them."

When Aunt Ora realized what she had said, the whole family laughed with her. Daddy promised her he would do whatever he could to fill the holes with gravel.

One might wonder how we had fun in spite of being so isolated. How did we overcome our fears? Children don't always need lots of gadgets to amuse themselves. During most of our childhood, I remember our having one bicycle, a tricycle, a red wagon, and one doll. We had checkers, dominos, rubber balls, and jigsaw puzzles. Small toys, including whistles, yo-yos, harmonicas, and spinning tops, were also available. We took turns and shared everything.

"For Ruth and me, the youngest girls, situations were somewhat different," Yvonne recalled. "One Christmas each of us got a doll. I also got a little cow on rollers that went 'Moo' as it raised its head. We were happy to have a toy to call our own."

Many times, we improvised to have fun. For jump ropes, we used rope that Daddy had for the farm animals. We shortened them or just cut them in half. Sometimes we wrapped the excess rope around our wrists to make it shorter.

Not having balls didn't hinder us when playing dodge or baseball. We simply wrapped twine around rags to form balls. We also used tin cans instead of balls, sticks for bats, and pieces of board to mark the bases.

The month of March was usually a great time to fly kites. We tried time after time to make kites but were never able to get the right materials. Strips of wood and the paper we used never worked.

During the summer, we had fun with June bugs that were caught and kept in jars. They didn't bite, so they weren't harmful. Thread, which Mama used for sewing, was tied around the bugs' legs. Having a bug flying around with a long piece of thread attached was fun to watch.

Summer wasn't fun if we didn't make mud pies. Using berries from pokeweed plants, we made blueberry pies, which we sat on the fence posts to bake. We also used pokeberries as nail polish.

In early July, after the corn had grown silks, we gathered the silk, braided it, and made wigs for our doll.

Hopscotch was one of our favorite games. A bare area in the backyard was the perfect place for that.

I don't remember being bored or even hearing that word. When we had time for fun, it was appreciated. Daddy and Mama sometimes joined us for checkers. Daddy won most of those games.

Growing up and having more experiences at school, at church, and in the community, made us less fearful of so many things. We made new friends at school, went on fieldtrips, and got involved in various activities. Attending church gave us opportunities to mingle with other children, participate in youth activities, and worship with other congregations.

We were permitted to ride our bicycle to the mailbox, which was located at the end of the dirt road by the highway, a mile away. We also rode to the country stores in Black Creek. The more experiences we had outside the home, the more confidence we developed in dealing with people and the community around us.

THE LOST SHOE

Listen to my prayer; rescue me as you promised.
Psalm 120:170

After moving to the Beale farm in December, we were excited about attending Damascus School. Our cousins and many of our friends from church attended that school.

The first day of school after Christmas break was the day after New Year's Day. Unfortunately, my first day attending the new school was much later than that of my sisters.

One day in late December while my sisters and I were in the barn getting corn to feed the animals, one of my shoes came off and was covered by falling corn that had been piled up to the loft. To make matters worse, when I tried to find it, more ears fell and buried it deeper.

"My shoe in under the corn," I said.

"Your shoe in under the corn? What happened to it?" one of them asked.

"It just came off my foot and when I tried to get it, I couldn't find it. No matter how much I dig, I just can't find it," I cried.

It was so cold in the barn that after helping me look for a while, we decided to look for it later.

"We have to help you find it tomorrow. I'm freezing," one of them said as we went to the house.

The next day and many days thereafter, my sisters tried to help me. No shoe. We just couldn't find it. It was difficult for Mama and Daddy to help look for it.

"I can't help you," Daddy said. "I have to get up at daybreak and go to work."

Usually in December and January, farm chores slacked off, so Daddy sometimes put in long hours at a basket factory or wherever he could find work. It was dark each day by the time he got home—too late to look for shoes in the barn unless he used a flashlight.

Mama had so much to do around the house with three younger children to care for that she didn't have time to help.

"I have to take care of Eileen, Ernell, and Yvonne," she said. "They can't be left alone in this house. Something might happen to them."

It would soon be the first day of school, and I was still missing my little brown shoe. I was so afraid I would have to miss that day. The more we dug, the more corn fell. It was still piled up to the loft. Sometimes we had to jump out of the way to avoid being buried under the piles.

Sadly, the first day of school came, and I still hadn't found my shoe. With tears in my eyes, I watched my sisters as they dressed, and Daddy took them to school. I dressed, put on Daddy's knee-high black rubber boots, and went to the barn alone in search of my shoe. I knew exactly where I was when it slipped off my foot. Each day, I searched the same area. More days passed. My fears grew. I won't ever go to school again. I won't pass to fourth grade. I'll have to be in third grade again next year. I'll always be a year behind my cousin, Louise and my sister Rebie. Everyone will just say I'm a dumbbell.

At night, I thought about where my shoe could be and hoped I would find it the next day. I kept thinking about the children at school. I wondered how the new school looked and what my teacher was like.

Each day when my sisters came home, they told me about the new school and said that my teacher asked about me.

"Where is the other little girl? When is she coming to school?" she asked.

Each day one of them answered, "She's at home. She can't find her shoe. She's still looking for it."

Since Rebie was also in third grade, I sat with her at night as she did her homework. We figured out answers in math together. I missed being able to read, write, and do math at school. Each night, I hoped, maybe tomorrow I will be really lucky and uncover my shoe.

One might wonder why I didn't have another pair of shoes or why my parents didn't go to town and buy new shoes. Our family had no money. Those weren't the best of times for us. No close relatives had extra money to help out either. The area didn't have thrift shops, the Salvation Army, Goodwill Industries, or places where we could get used or inexpensive shoes. Having eight girls in the family meant that each child had only one pair of shoes, which she wore every day until the shoes were worn out. By the end of the school year, we often had to put cardboard in them to cover the holes. Sometimes Daddy took them to the shoe shop and had new soles put on them.

During the summer, we rarely wore shoes when we were at home. Being without shoes was not a problem in the summer unless we were going someplace.

Perhaps my parents could have done more to make sure I had shoes. I sometimes wonder if letting me miss school and look for my shoes was their way of punishing me or trying to make me more responsible. As a youngster, I was somewhat daring and did lots of things I shouldn't have done.

New shoes weren't an option. As my sisters continued to go to school, I looked for my shoe. The two mules and the cow in the stables nearby stood silently each day as I entered the barn. They watched me as if puzzled by my being there. Occasionally, a field mouse squeaked and scampered by to avoid the falling corn. Thank God, I didn't see any snakes. My thoughts kept going back to the snake that we once saw in the hayloft on the Womble farm and the encounter that Rebie and I had with a snake in the pear tree. It was so cold that the snakes were probably hibernating, but that didn't keep me from worrying about them.

After many trips to the barn and what seemed like weeks of tossing ears of corn from one side to the other, I saw what looked like the heel of my shoe. There it was—deep down among the corn. I kept digging as the corn shifted. When I was finally able to get it, I yelled, "My shoe, my shoe. I've found my shoe."

I was so happy. I almost fell as I ran to the house in Daddy's boots to tell Mama. I could hardly wait until my sisters got home. When I saw them coming home, I jumped up and down. They knew right away what had happened.

"I found my shoe," I said. "I'm going to school tomorrow. I'll meet my teacher and the children in my classroom. My teacher won't have to ask, 'Where is the other little girl? When is she coming to school?' I am going to be in third grade at Damascus School, and I can hardly wait."

DAMASCUS SCHOOL

Pay close attention to what you hear. The closer you listen, the more understanding you will be given.
Mark 4:24

Daddy got up early, stoked the fire smoldering in the pot-bellied stove, and yelled, "Y'all get up now, so you won't be late for school."

Mama got up, cooked oatmeal for breakfast, and made egg biscuits for our lunch. I was already awake and had been for a while after sleeping with my shoes by the bed. Our hair had been neatly braided, and our clothes had been chosen the night before. It was going to be my first day at Damascus School.

Getting to school was an ordeal. It was five miles away. Having to walk to school was too far, especially for Minnie and me, but sometimes we walked anyway. On most cold or rainy days, Daddy took us to school. Many days for various reasons, we just stayed home.

When everyone was ready to go, we all got into the car and off we went. Soon we arrived at school. Up the steep steps we walked. Elizabeth and Ruby went to Mrs. Spencer's room with grades 4-7 while Rebie, Minnie, and I went to Miss Langston's room with grades 1-3.

Damascus school was much like Rosenwald—two large rooms, big windows that stretched almost to the ceilings, long chalkboards, and pot-bellied stoves. A slate board divided the two rooms. It could be removed to make one large area for group activities and programs.

Our classroom was arranged with rows of iron and wooden desks attached to the floor. All desks faced the chalkboards. First graders were in the row near Miss Langston's desk, second graders were in the middle row, and third graders were in a row near the cloakroom.

As I walked to her desk, Miss Langston said, "Good morning, I am so glad to see you."

"Good morning, Miss Langston," I said.

"You must be Daphine."

I nodded my head. "Yes, Miss Langston."

I was too timid to correct her. It's Daphne, Daphne Louise Harris. Hasn't anyone ever heard the name Daphne before? I must really be the only Daphne in the world. I wondered why Mama let Miss Esther give me that name.

Pointing to a desk at the front of the room near Rebie, Miss Langston said, "Daphine, you can sit in front of your sister."

From that day on, everyone in that area called me Daphine, instead of Daphne.

The time spent in third grade seems to have passed quickly. What I remember most about it was learning multiplication and division. Math was my favorite subject.

Night after night, we practiced, "One times two is two. Two times two is four. Four times two is eight," until we knew all the facts. Long division was the most difficult, but with lots of help at home, I learned how to do it.

Despite missing many days of school because of my lost shoe, I was promoted at the end of the school year. Both Rebie and I went to fourth grade.

When school opened the following September, we were assigned to Mrs. Spencer's room. Fourth grade was like middle school. Grades 4-7 were in the same room. That meant Elizabeth, Ruby, Rebie, and I were in the same classroom. Having four girls from the same family together must have been difficult for Mrs. Spencer. She got us mixed up and for some time, didn't know one girl from the other.

A typical school day began with Mrs. Spencer standing on the steps ringing the brass school bell. The pupils got in straight lines—girls in one line and boys in the other. The children said, "Good morning, Mrs. Spencer," as they walked quietly into the building.

Devotions involved singing patriotic songs, repeating The Lord's Prayer and the pledge to the flag.

"Stand straight and face the flag," she said. "Put your right hand over your heart and your left hand beside you. Now repeat with me."

"I pledge allegiance to the flag of the United States of America and to the Republic for which it stands, one Nation, indivisible with liberty and justice for all."

The words "under God" were added to the pledge on June 14, 1954, after being approved by President Dwight D. Eisenhower.

Sometimes we sang religious songs and recited Bible verses. Most of us had Bibles in the home but didn't know lots of Bible verses. We heard the same short verses most of the time.

"Thou shall not kill."

"Thou shall not steal."

"Remember the Sabbath day and keep it holy."

"The Lord is my shepherd, I shall not want."

Sometimes, being silly, some of the boys said under their breath, "Jesus wept, Moses slept."

Their responses caused giggling among the rest of the class and annoyed our teacher. She usually punished them by paddling them in their hands or making them miss recess.

I listened to everything that Mrs. Spencer taught. It didn't matter what grade or subject she was teaching. Sometimes she let me work with the upper grades, especially during reading.

I can still remember the poetry we learned. Around the first of every month, Mrs. Spencer wrote poems on the chalkboard. Some of them were short, and others like "The Night Before Christmas" were long.

"Copy these poems and learn to recite them," she instructed.

Sometimes it took forever to copy them. Before we could barely finish one, she erased the board to write another. Before the end of the month, she checked to make sure we had learned them. Each pupil had to stand in front of the class and recite the poetry of the month.

"Copying the poetry was not a problem for me," Minnie said. "I enjoyed writing. I can recall the time that the superintendent of schools visited the classroom and complimented me on how well I could write."

Unlike years later, no televisions or other audiovisual materials were in the classroom. Radios were used when special events took place. I remember presidential inaugurations and State of the Union addresses, which we had to listen to, take notes on, and report to the class. I also remember listening to the coronation of Queen Elizabeth II of England on the radio.

We had no books to read at home except the textbooks that were purchased for use at school. The county didn't provide free textbooks, the school didn't have a library, and the county didn't have public libraries that Negro children could use. I really don't know if the county had a public library for any of its citizens. All schools and county facilities were still segregated. White students were bused to consolidated schools while Negro students walked or were bused to small one- or two-room schools. We didn't have access to a school library until high school. I never went to a public library until I was in college in Norfolk, VA.

Mrs. Spencer required us to purchase subscriptions to *Weekly Reader* and *Current Events*, which were weekly publications that kept us aware of news around the world. Educational materials of that type enhanced our skills in reading, science, and social studies I enjoyed learning about people in faraway places.

We had access to newspapers that we read at home. We especially liked the comics. For us, they were somewhat like soap operas are today. We couldn't wait to get home from school to read about what happened in "Blondie" and "Dick Tracy."

Mrs. Spencer was a capable teacher. If one considers the conditions under which she had to teach, she probably should have been commended. She taught us valuable skills that impact our lives today.

The one habit my teacher had that I disliked was the way she addressed children when they exhibited unacceptable behavior. During that time, children could be spanked, and a lot of that took place. Most of the time after scolding or spanking the children, Mrs. Spencer just looked at them and said, "You're just a nuisance."

What a great way to lower a child's self-esteem. For a long time, I didn't know the meaning of the word "nuisance," and that it could be so demeaning. Teachers always seemed to use big words that we didn't understand. Several children from the

Newsom family, especially the boys, sometimes needed to be reprimanded. Until I learned the meaning of the word, I thought she was referring to one of them. So, the day she called me to her desk and after talking to me said, "You're just a nuisance," I didn't understand what she was saying. I actually thought she said, "Newsom" and had gotten me mixed up with one of the Newsom girls. I still can't remember what I had done. I wanted to say, "I'm not a Newsom. I'm a Harris."

The nine of us went to Damascus School. Ernell seems to have had more difficulty learning to read than the rest of us. Her getting burned at an early age and having to spend so much time in hospitals might have accounted for that. In the beginning, reading was so hard for her. When trying to remember words by sight, she needed lots of help. All of us tried to assist. Daddy even tried to help. We all remember the time when he was listening to her read as she got to the word "that" and just couldn't say it. After pausing and with lots of frustration in his voice, he said, "The word is that. Say that."

When Ernell responded by saying, "say that," we knew she didn't have a clue what she was trying to read. I think Daddy realized she needed much more assistance than we could give. Nevertheless, we continued to help. With more attention from her teacher, Miss Langston, she was able to progress. She made up for time lost while recovering from the accident and did well.

After walking to and from school many, many days, the county sent Daddy a letter indicating that the system would assist us with transportation.

"The county is going to pay me to take y'all to school," he said, after opening the letter.

The county had decided to pay Daddy 15 cents per day, per child, which amounted to about 75 cents per day and less than $150 for the entire year. He was paid during the summer after the school year ended.

"That's not much, but it's better than nothing," he said. "There won't be no more walking ten miles a day to and from school."

Of course, we continued to walk many days. Sometimes Daddy was too busy, his old car needed to be repaired, or he didn't have enough gas. On warm days, we didn't mind walking, especially after school. It gave us a chance to mingle with other children. We could also stop at the country store and buy candy and cookies as we passed through the Black Creek area. Candy and cookies could be purchased for one cent each. If we were lucky enough to find a discarded soda bottle, we could get a refund of three cents.

I imagine the decision to pay to transport us to school was because of the Separate But Equal Doctrine that was law in the segregated schools of the South during that time. School districts could maintain segregated facilities as long as they provided the same or equal services for all students. Paying Daddy to transport us to school was probably proof that transportation was available for us just as that provided with the yellow school buses for other children.

During that time, the county must have been making special efforts to make sure all children were attending school regularly. New classmates from a large family began school. They lived a great distance from school, also. Some of them were teenagers and were said to have never attended school. Most of them were placed in Mrs. Spencer's room because they were too big for the small desks in the lower classroom.

It was difficult for them to make the adjustment. It was equally hard for the rest of the class. Instead of trying to discipline them, Mrs. Spencer sent for their parents. One day when their mother was contacted, she came to school. She didn't wait to take them home for punishment. She didn't even take time to go to the nearby woods to get keen switches. After she ripped a slat off the back of the school building, they were reprimanded right there on the school grounds. I don't remember their parents having to come to school again. Somehow, Mrs. Spencer and all of us endured those difficult days.

Years later, while Yvonne and Ruth continued to attend Damascus School, bus transportation was provided. "A yellow school bus driven by Mr. Darden picked us up at the beginning of the dirt road where we lived," Yvonne recalled. "We still had to walk a mile to get to the bus stop because the road was not maintained by the county."

After spending four years in Mrs. Spencer's room, all of us, except Ruth, went to high school in the city of Franklin, VA. No more sitting in one classroom the entire day or long walks just to get to school. We looked forward to riding the yellow school buses, which were provided for all high school students. We were also excited about meeting new friends and experiencing life beyond Damascus school and the farming communities of Black Creek and Burdette.

A Trip to the Country Store

In your majesty, ride out to victory, defending truth, humility and justice. Go forth and perform awe-inspiring deeds.
Psalm 45:4

The Beale farm was located near the community of Black Creek, which was about four miles away. Three stores and train tracks seemed to equally divide the area. On one side of the tracks were two stores and several houses. One store sold clothes, shoes, straw hats, and farm supplies. The other sold groceries. Eggs and chickens could be bought or sold at that store.

The market on the opposite side of the tracks sold groceries, gasoline, kerosene, and farm supplies. About as many houses were on that side as on the other side of the tracks.

When we were old enough to ride longer distances on our bicycle, Mama allowed two of us to go to one of the stores to get items she needed. One child pedaled the bike while the other rode on the back seat.

"Y'all be careful and watch out for the traffic," she said. "Sometimes those cars and trucks move so fast. If you see a big truck coming, stop the bike and stand by the side of the road until it passes. And don't let nobody give you a ride unless you know them."

The trip I remember most was the day Mama let Ruby and me take two chickens to the store to sell.

"Y'all go out in the yard and catch two chickens," she said. "Put them in a bag and tie it with a piece of twine, so they won't fly out."

Using corn kernels as bait, we got two of the fattest hens that we could catch. "Here chick, chick, chick," we called as we grabbed them. By today's standards, they would most likely be called free range or organic chickens.

We put them in a burlap bag and off we went. Ruby pedaled the bike as I rode on the back seat and tried with all my might to hold the bag of chickens, as well as the seat of the bike. I must have been about nine years old, and Ruby was probably eleven. We had to sell the chickens and make purchases from a list Mama gave us. She sometimes had us buy items like Super Suds, Rinso, Ivory Soap, cheese, oatmeal, and rice.

It was one of the hottest days that summer. The temperature must have been in the 90s. I don't know why we didn't go to the store before it got so hot.

We wore wide-brimmed straw hats that we secured tightly under our chins to protect us from the hot sun. Every summer, Daddy made sure all of us had straw hats to use when doing chores in the fields. He went shopping at the country store and bought one for each of us. The hats had colorful bands, and we were eager to pick our favorite color. Having different colors made it easy for each sister to identify her hat.

The heat made the chickens uncomfortable. Bwok, bwok, bwok, bwok, bwok, they clucked, jumping around in the bag frantically trying to get out. They moved around so much as we rode along that one chicken fell on each side of the wheels of the bike. Although that sort of balanced the load, I was afraid they would get caught in the spokes of the wheels. I also thought that being inside the thick burlap bag on such a hot and humid day would cause them to suffocate and die. I prayed, "Lord, please let these chickens live until we get to the store. Don't let them die in this bag before we get there."

Ruby pedaled the bike as fast as she could—past the open fields where farmers were busy tending their crops, past animals that briefly stopped grazing to watch us as we cruised by. Uphill and down we went, being careful to stay out of the way of traffic and trying to make sure we didn't veer off the side of the country road. As long as the chickens were moving, I knew they were alive. If they stopped moving for a second, I panicked.

About half way there, the chickens got quiet. No jumping! No scratching! No clucking! Visions of two dead chickens flashed before my eyes.

"God, I hope these chickens aren't dead," I said as I felt the bag.

We stopped briefly, put the bag on the ground, and attempted to see if the chickens were still alive. As soon as we opened the bag and they got a breath of fresh air, they tried to fly out.

"Thank God, they're still alive," I said.

We quickly closed the bag, mounted the bike, and continued to ride as fast as we could. The country store was not far away. "We can make it. We can make it," I said.

When we finally reached the country store, the chickens were still trying to free themselves. We parked our bike, put the kickstand down, and went into the store. Inside, the store must have been like going into stores of the Wild West. It was so dark and drab that it actually looked abandoned.

"This store looks empty," I said. "I don't see nobody."

I was barely tall enough to see over the counter. We saw no one. Since the door wasn't locked, we knew that someone must have been minding the store.

As we plopped the bag on the counter, the storekeeper appeared. "We have two chickens to sell," I said.

With a surprised look on his face, he peered at us and said, "Whose boys are y'all?"

We were so bashful and timid that we didn't bother to tell him we were girls. We were taught to be polite and courteous when grownups talked to us, so we politely said, "Mr. Herbert Harris's."

The darkness must have obstructed the storekeeper's view from behind the counter because we certainly weren't dressed like boys. We usually wore skirts or dresses. I don't remember girls wearing pants during that time.

"What kind of chickens are these?" he asked.

"Two hens," we answered, speaking at the same time.

"Rhode Island Reds," I said.

With that, the storekeeper took the chickens to the back of the store and weighed them. After putting them in a chicken coop, he collected the items from Mama's list and gave us some change. I don't remember what we got that day or how much change we were given. I was just happy that we didn't end up with two dead chickens when we got to the store.

The bike ride home was much less stressful. Not having to worry about the chickens was quite a relief. I thought about the storekeeper and what he said to us.

"That man thought we were boys." Ruby chuckled.

"He asked, 'whose boys are y'all?'"

We didn't understand. Why did he want to know who we were? Perhaps he needed to know the farmer from whom he was purchasing chickens.

It didn't matter that he didn't know we were girls. What he really didn't know was, we were the new girls in the community. We were Herbert and Annie's girls. We were just two of the nine.

We could hardly wait until we got home to tell the family what happened. They didn't understand why the storekeeper thought we were boys.

As time passed, it wasn't uncommon to see two of us on a blue bike, the only one we owned, going to and from the country stores in Black Creek. People in the community learned that we had only girls in our family. No one ever referred to us as boys again.

DADDY'S CARS

My grace is all you need.
My power works best in weakness.
2 Corinthians 12:9

As long as I can remember, Daddy had some type of automobile. He couldn't afford new vehicles. Used cars were purchased instead. I remember his owning Model T and Model A Fords, which must have really been old for him to be driving them in the forties. He also owned a 1939 Chevrolet, a 1948 or 1949 Ford, and a 1973 Ford Galaxy 500.

Safety regulations for motor vehicles in the state of Virginia during that time must not have existed because Daddy's cars always seemed to have some parts that didn't function properly. Tires were forever going flat, and one of his cars had holes in the floorboard that he sometimes covered with cardboard. His old two-door coupe had doors, which sometimes automatically swung open as he made turns or drove around curves.

The holes in the floorboards sometimes proved to be convenient for us when Mama and Daddy took us to town late evenings, especially on Saturdays. Too young to be left home alone, we stayed in the car for hours while they shopped, made visits to doctors, or Daddy got a haircut. We were under strict orders not to get out of the car. The town had no public restrooms. Negroes couldn't always use restrooms in the stores, and no trashcans were along the streets. We had to wait until we got home or stop along the way and use the wooded areas or cornfields.

Young children couldn't always control themselves. So, when nature called, and with cries of "I got to go, I got to go, I can't hold it," we used the holes in the floorboard of the car to take care of personal needs. We didn't hesitate to use them. I imagine the street sweepers weren't happy campers the next morning when they saw evidence of Daddy's car having been parked on the street and our being in it for a long time.

As the family grew, getting Mama and the nine of us in the car was a real challenge. The family was too big for us to ride safely and comfortably in the vehicle. We took turns going to church, to town, or just to visit family and friends. Daddy was the only driver until I got my driver's license. Mama never got a license even though she knew how to drive both the car and the tractor.

Sometimes, all of us had to be together in the car, such as the time when everyone had to be taken to the Public Health Department to get polio vaccinations. I don't imagine anyone ever thought to schedule some of us to get the shots on different days. Perhaps the county officials just didn't know how many children were in the family. That day, we were stuffed in the car like sardines in a can. The four older girls sat on the back seat. Minnie, Ernell, Eileen, and Yvonne sat on the laps of the older ones or stood behind the front seats. Mama, Daddy, and Ruth rode in the front seat.

When the department finished with us that day, I imagine they knew exactly how many girls were in our family. Most of us had never had shots, except for the pricks of the skin when we were vaccinated for smallpox prior to beginning school. So, we were afraid.

When we saw those huge syringes, which looked like those we'd seen Daddy use on the horse and mules, the screaming began. It didn't matter that Daddy kept saying, "Be quiet, stand still, stop that hollering, and shut your mouth." The crying continued until each child got vaccinated.

I imagine the staff was awfully glad to see us with our runny noses get in the car and leave. It was an uncomfortable trip, but we got shots and went home with sad faces and sore arms.

Another time, when the circus came to the nearby town of Ivor, Daddy came home excited. He had seen tents, rides, and refreshment stands being prepared and clowns and animals, practicing for their acts.

"Y'all get ready," he said. "I'm going to take y'all to Ivor to the circus. I just watched them unloading a lot of animals off big trucks. They got some of the biggest elephants that I've ever seen. I saw lions and tigers, too. This is the only day that we can go. So, you need to hurry."

The area was still racially segregated. Blacks could attend activities of that nature only on designated days.

Thank God, seat belt regulations hadn't started because again, all of us piled into the car for the trip. No one thought twice about how uncomfortable the ride would be. We wanted to see all of the animals Daddy talked about.

Seeing the lions, tigers, and elephants was exciting. The clowns made us laugh as Daddy treated us to cotton candy. We were amazed at how big and strong the elephants looked. That was our first experience visiting a circus—a memorable one indeed.

On a trip years later, as Daddy was driving to town, something unbelievable happened. Most of the younger girls were in the car that day. Some of the children sat, and others stood behind the front seats. Eileen, whom we called Argie, was standing behind the front passenger's seat where Mama was seated. As Daddy made a left turn down the main road to Franklin, the right door of the old car swung open and out fell Eileen. Mama was so accustomed to the door opening that she closed it immediately while looking straight ahead. She didn't realize she was missing one of her girls. The rest of them must have been too traumatized to speak. No one cried. No one screamed. Not a sound was made. They simply sat with their eyes glazed as if they were in a trance and didn't say a word.

Shortly after Daddy had safely made his turn and was headed down the straight road, he glanced in the rearview mirror and saw someone running frantically trying to catch the car. After taking a closer look, he said, "Who's that? Who is that running behind the car? Is that Argie?"

Mama looked back and noticed that one child was missing. "Lord, have mercy. That's Argie," she said. "Herbert, when that door swung open, she must have fell out, and we didn't even know it."

After Daddy slowed the car down, Mama said she could tell by the look on Daddy's face that it was hard for him to believe what he saw. He had left his child in the middle of the road, and neither he nor she had seen her tumble out of the car. He brought the car to a screeching stop, quickly got out, ran, picked up Eileen, and headed straight to Franklin to the local hospital.

Eileen had scrapes and scratches on her face and arms and a large bruise on her forehead. Pieces of sand and gravel had become embedded in the bruises when she hit the pavement as she fell out of the car. Her crying frightened the whole family.

"Why didn't y'all say something? Didn't y'all see her fall out of the car?" Mama asked.

With all the crying, everyone still seemed to be so afraid that they didn't know how to answer her question.

Daddy couldn't get the old car to go fast enough. Even though the hospital was only four miles away, it seemed like he would never get there.

At the hospital, the doctors examined Eileen and assured our parents that she hadn't sustained any broken bones or major injuries, so she was allowed to go home.

Except for having a scar on her forehead for a long time, she recovered from her injuries physically. I'm not sure that she has fully recovered from the trauma of the mishap because she continues to be afraid of riding in cars that are moving fast or going up and down steep hills.

I don't know what Daddy did to the doors of the car after that day. I don't remember the door swinging open again, and certainly that was the first and the last time anyone fell out of a car while he was driving. For a long time, when we passed the area on that road, that incident came to mind and was mentioned.

When we get together and discuss old times, we make light of what happened and say that everyone was quiet that day because they were tired of being cramped in the car and were relieved to have more room in the back seat.

THE BEAR HUNT

Fear gripped me and my bones trembled.
Job 4:14

Once in a while on the farm, unusual things happened that caused a lot of excitement and concern like the day Daddy went bear hunting. Before that day, he had only hunted small game, such as rabbits and squirrels. He had never hunted large game like deer and bears. Deer were plentiful, but bears were never seen in the area.

I don't think Daddy was a skillful hunter although he had a single-barreled shotgun, which was kept in a corner of a room in the house or mounted above his and Mama's bedroom door. He rarely brought home anything when he went hunting. The few rabbits and squirrels that he killed were usually mangled.

He had dogs that he attempted to train. The dogs I remember the most were Brownie and Rover. Brownie was part Beagle, and Rover was probably a mixture of many breeds. They were quite docile and about as skillful at hunting as our father. They were good for barking to let us know someone was approaching the house, and that was about all.

The bear hunt took place early one spring morning. I remember it vividly. The warm sun shone brightly. In the nearby forest, the dogwood trees were in bloom, and signs of spring were everywhere. As we played in the yard, suddenly a lone black animal was spotted walking near the edge of the woods around what had been a peanut field. It was unlike any animal we had seen in that part of Southampton County. It looked as though it had not eaten for a long time. Its shaggy matted coat seemed to hang loosely to its gaunt body.

Was it some kind of animal that has hibernated all winter and was just coming out of hiding with the beginning of spring to look for food?

Brownie and Rover began to howl and bark. Their actions let us know that something was quite unusual about the creature that had suddenly appeared in the area.

We hollered for Daddy to come outside. "Look. What's that walking around the field? What kind of animal is that?" I asked.

"I don't know what that is," Daddy answered, trying to get a better view of what we saw.

As all of us gazed in awe, one of Daddy's friends stopped by for a visit. Right away, his attention was directed toward the animal that continued to make its way near the edge of the field.

Daddy's friend stuttered when he tried to conduct a normal conversation. When he became excited, it was extremely difficult to understand what he was saying. The wad of chewing tobacco or the dip of snuff he usually had in his mouth made matters worse.

As soon as Daddy's friend saw the creature, he said, "Ha-Ha-Ha Hubbut, da-da-da-da that's a ha-ha hog bear."

Even though dad's name was Herbert Harris, most of the locals just called him Hubbut. He didn't mind being called Hubbut. He had been called names worse than that. Once, when one of our neighbors was having a mental breakdown she greeted him with a name, which was totally different and quite a surprise.

"Well, how are you Mr. Harry's Ass?" she asked, one day when Daddy stopped by. He couldn't believe what he heard but didn't try to correct her.

"That's a ha-ha hog bear Ha-Ha-Ha Hubbut," said Daddy's friend as we continued to gaze. "I-I know. I know. Ha-Ha Hog bear is good meat! Ha-Ha Hog bear is good meat. We ou-ou-ou ought to go ha-ha-ha hunting and k-k-kill it. Ha-Ha Hog bear is good meat. Ha-Ha Hog bear is good meat!"

We had heard of black bears being spotted in the Great Dismal Swamp and Suffolk areas, which were about 40 miles away, but not hog bears. When we were children, the mention of a bear frightened us. We were afraid to even go for a ride in the car through those areas, especially at night. We thought the car might stall or have a flat tire, and that would be the end for us.

Even though Daddy said he had never seen nor heard of a hog bear, he was so easy going that it wasn't hard to be convinced that hunting the bear was a good idea. His friend was an older man. So, I'm sure seniority also helped to sway our father.

Daddy got his shotgun and some extra shells. He whistled for his dogs, and off they went. Since he had only one gun, I guess his friend went along to help him bring the bear home.

The animal had already disappeared. Soon Brownie and Rover entered the woods ahead of Daddy and his friend. As we stood watching, we could hear the dogs barking as if they were following the scent of the animal. The sound became louder and louder. We expected to hear gunfire at any moment. For a while, the barks seemed far away. Then they seemed to be getting closer. We became so afraid that we took shelter inside.

As we peered out the windows, I worried about how some of our family's daily routines might have to change if bears were in the area.

Life for us kids will certainly have to change. No more walking through the woods to see the beautiful dogwood trees in bloom in the spring. When we walk to school on days because Daddy can't take us, it'll be too dangerous to stop by the stream to watch tadpoles grow into frogs. How afraid I'll be when going with Great-Grandma Rindy to pick wild blueberries during the summer—one of my favorite outings.

We continued to watch, wait, and ponder. If they kill that bear, we'll have to eat it. When Daddy goes hunting, Mama cooks whatever he brings home. If she doesn't know how to cook it, she'll go straight to Great-Grandma's and have her tell her what to do.

Maybe Daddy's friend would like it. He can take it home for his family. Maybe they will eat it. I can ask his daughter if she liked it when I see her at school. I know she will tell me exactly how bear tastes.

After what seemed like hours, we saw Rover and Brownie come out of the woods panting after the long hunt. Shortly thereafter, Daddy and his friend appeared. They walked to the house slowly without ever looking back. With our faces pressed against the windowpanes, we looked for the bear. We didn't see the bear.

Did Daddy decide not to shoot the bear? Did Rover and Brownie lose scent of the bear and weren't able to track it? Or had the bear been too smart and was still out there in the woods?

Soon Brownie and Rover got to the house. They trotted straight to a nearby trough for a cool drink of water and later found a place to rest in the front yard under the large oak tree. When Daddy and his friend got to the house, they looked tired as they flopped down on the porch to rest. We ran outside to see what happened.

"Daddy, Daddy, where's the bear? Did you catch it? Did you kill it?"

We all had questions.

"Is it still in the woods?"

Daddy could probably tell by the looks on our faces that we were still quite frightened. He hung his head, chuckled, and said sheepishly, "Y'all girls don't have to be afraid. What we saw wasn't a bear. The animal we were hunting was just an old black dog. There are no bears around here."

By that time, Mama had come outside to find out what happened.

"A stray dog?" she asked, as she shook her head. "All that time, you couldn't tell that was a dog?"

Daddy's friend shook his head and stuttered his way out of his embarrassment.

"Ha-Ha-Ha Hubbut, I-I-I sure thought that was a ha-ha hog bear! Ha-Ha Hog bear is good meat! Ha-Ha Hog bear is good meat!"

We learned later that hog bear was the name used locally for a small variety of black bear found in Northern Florida, Georgia, and some of the Midwestern United States. No sightings of hog bears were reported in the area during that time. After that experience, I don't remember Daddy going hunting again.

COME SUNDAY

Remember to observe the Sabbath day
by keeping it holy.
Exodus 20:8

That morning, as we saw Mr. Dillard, the preacher, going down the path near where we lived, we couldn't believe what we were seeing. His horse-drawn wagon was filled with dried peanut vines, which were used to feed his livestock.

"Hey, Mr. Dillard," I shouted. "You should be on your way to church. Don't you know the devil's going to get you for hauling vines on Sunday? Don't you know you shouldn't be working today?"

Luckily, he was too far away to hear me.

For many years, the fourth commandment was strictly enforced in our family. On Sunday, all work ceased. No work in the fields, no washing, no ironing. Working was considered a sin if done on Sunday. On that day, it was expected that everyone went to church. Of course, most of us went, but the car didn't have enough room, so some of us stayed home. We took turns and argued or fussed about who went to church the last Sunday or who should go the next Sunday. Even if we didn't go, we certainly weren't expected to be seen working in the fields like Mr. Dillard.

The family attended Cedar Grove Baptist, which was about six miles away. It was an ordinary little church with a steeple and a cross at the top. A cedar tree grew in front of it. Like most churches in rural areas, it was built near a river, which was used for baptismal ceremonies years ago. Ruby and Elizabeth were baptized there. Later, a pool for baptismal services was installed in the church.

Right beside the church, which continues to serve the community, is a cemetery. Old tombstones mark the area where many of our ancestors, which include Grandpa Eddie and Grandma Nora, are buried. For many years on Memorial Day, Daddy made sure that the gravesites, for family members who didn't have gravestones were reshaped. He knew where each grave was located and could tell who was buried there. All the graves were decorated. Sometimes we used flowers that grew in our yard. They seemed to bloom just in time for that day.

The pastor, Reverend George Wiley Johnson, was a robust man with a loud booming voice. Upon seeing this typical preacher and hearing his voice, one would probably assume right away that his sermons could set the church on fire. He was known for belting out, "Oh Glory" or "Great God Almighty" at high points in his sermons. He also admonished the congregation by saying, "Don't do as I do. Do as I say."

He drove beautiful cars—always a large black one. He gave us rides sometimes if he happened to be in the area as we walked to and from school.

"Y'all want a ride? Hop in here," he said.

He drove awfully fast and always seemed to be in a hurry. When he got to the dirt road, he let us out to walk the rest of the way. I don't imagine he wanted to drive his car down that bumpy road.

After some of us moved away, and we had fewer mouths to feed, Reverend Johnson was sometimes invited to dinner.

"Boy, could he eat," Ernell, recalled. "Mama usually cooked fried chicken, country ham, string beans, potato salad, hot rolls, and chocolate cake. The grownups were served first. After eating, Reverend Johnson came outside and played jump rope or participated in whatever games we were playing. Later, he ate again. We were afraid there wouldn't be enough food left for us."

For years, church services were held on the second and fourth Sundays. Sunday school was held every Sunday. Reverend

Johnson was pastor of three churches. I imagine that was the reason why he always seemed to be rushing. Trying to serve three congregations was probably not an easy task.

The whole family participated in church activities. We attended Sunday school, and as each of us became old enough, we sang in the Junior Choir. Mama sang in the Senior Choir and was active in many fund-raising activities. If she didn't raise the most money, she wasn't happy.

The church served our spiritual needs, as well as enhanced our cultural experiences. During the summer, we attended vacation Bible school and looked forward to trips that were sponsored. We were chosen to attend Baptist conventions, where we had to keep journals and make reports to the congregation at our church the following Sunday.

We had outings to Sea View Beach, which was located in the Great Neck area of Virginia Beach. That was one of the few area beaches that Blacks were allowed to use. We packed lunches that usually consisted of fried chicken or ham sandwiches, which wouldn't spoil quickly. Very few places were along the way where we could stop for food. White-owned restaurants sometimes served Blacks from separate entrances at the back or side of the establishments. We rarely had extra money to spend for food, so we avoided that type of discrimination.

We also took trips to Washington, D.C. to visit the National Zoo and to Colonial Williamsburg to attend the outdoor drama, *Common Glory.*

A trip to Skyline Drive was touted as a great opportunity to see the Blue Ridge Mountains and be at an elevation so high that we could wash our faces in the clouds. We could also visit Luray

Caverns and see rock formations shaped like an egg cooked sunny-side up.

Those experiences helped to broaden our knowledge of the world outside our community. That also gave us something to share in September when returning to school and having to write an essay on, "How I Spent My Summer Vacation."

After several years of attending the church, Daddy was asked to serve on the Board of Deacons. Getting home from church one Sunday he said, "Annie Mae, Reverend Johnson asked me to become a deacon today."

"And what did you tell him?"

"I said I would do it. That's all right with me. I will do the best I can."

I don't know how long it took, but Daddy was ordained and served on the board the rest of his life. That group was held in high esteem in the church, as well as in the community. They sat together in what was called the "Amen Corner." The pastor and congregation could depend on them for support. They were often called on to pray and assist with offerings, baptismal ceremonies, and Holy Communion.

Most of the deacons had their own style of prayer. If we listened to them often, we knew exactly what they were going to say, what they were thankful for, and everyone they wanted blessed. Said with a mournful voice, a typical prayer went somewhat like this:

> Let us pray.
> Heavenly Father, we come before you today with
> bowed heads and humble hearts thanking you for
> the blessings that you have bestowed upon us.

Thank you, O God, for last night's rest and the angels that watched over us while we slept.
Thank you for protecting us from all hurt, harm, and danger.
And, Heavenly Father, thank you for waking us up this morning. You woke us up and started us on our way, O God. You woke us up to a day that we have never seen before. And this day, O Father, once it is gone, will never be seen again.

Lord, thank you for putting food on our tables this morning.
Thank you for the clothes on our backs and the roof over our heads.
Heavenly Father, we're asking you to bless the poor and needy. Have mercy on those that know you and those that know you not.
Visit the sick, the shut-ins, and those in the nursing homes and the hospitals. Comfort them with your healing power, O God. Let them know that there is power, power in your name. Let them know there is healing in your name.

Bless our pastor, O God. Be with him as he preaches the Word this morning. Bless our church family and all church families around the world. Go with us and stand by us, O God, all the days of our lives.

And, Heavenly Father, when we have gone the last mile of the way and this world can't afford us a home any longer, give us a home in your kingdom where we can praise your holy name forever more.

These and other blessings we ask in Thy name. Amen

One Sunday during the summer, Children's Day was observed at church. On that day, the youth participated in the services. The Junior Choir sang while other young people recited poems and participated in plays or other activities. Girls wore white dresses. Prior to that day, Mama usually got a letter from Aunt Ora.

"I will be there on Saturday morning," she wrote. "Have Herbert pick me up at the bus station in Franklin. I bought white dresses for each of the girls."

Later, after getting a car, she drove from Norfolk early Sunday morning. Sure enough, when she got there, dresses for the nine of us had been purchased and placed neatly in her bags. Later after taking sewing classes and becoming skillful at using a sewing machine, she made our clothes. She was a kind and loving aunt, who had no children of her own and supported us as long as she lived.

"I sure hope y'all can wear these dresses," she said. "Y'all try them on. Annie Mae, we might have to put hems in some of them."

We weren't concerned about how they fit. We were just happy to have new clothes for that Sunday. Mama and Aunt Ora beamed with pride as we, dressed in frilly dresses, were called to recite our parts in the program. Some of us were too bashful to participate.

Many of the older members wanted to see the nine of us together. They said, "Annie Mae, you got all your churen here today? Get 'em together, so we can see 'em."

One of the male members looked at us and said, "I want to have a lot of churen just like Hubbut."

He got his wish. He had 13 children, but they weren't all girls.

In late August and early September, all of the local churches conducted weeklong services that they called "The Meeting." One service was held each day and another at night. Most members attended at night because many of them had to work during the day.

Thursday night was the most popular night. For those services, many people attended, including members from neighboring churches and relatives from out of town. That was when the most powerful preaching and most enjoyable singing took place. Sometimes it was standing room only.

During "The Meeting," most people who had not been baptized joined the church, especially children. Those who gave their lives to Christ and became candidates for baptism were referred to as "getting religion."

A guest minister conducted the services during which he usually threatened fire and brimstone or warned, "Your soul's going straight to hell when you die if you don't repent of your sins and be born again."

Shouts of "amen, preach, or yes sir " came from the deacons in the "Amen Corner."

Soon we heard "Yes Lord. Thank you Jesus. Hallelujah."

Then we saw a hat sail across the sanctuary. Members were said to be "Feeling the Spirit" or "Getting Happy."

"Oh Lord, that's Grandma's hat," I said.

We knew then if we didn't know before that Grandma Queen Esther was in the audience. When she felt the spirit, she grabbed her hat and threw it across the sanctuary like someone throwing a Frisbee. The ushers usually rushed over to comfort her. They also made sure that her hat was returned.

One of the ushers skipped around the church as she expressed her feelings in her own special way. A spry man jumped up and walked across the pews. The jumping and shouting sometimes frightened us.

As the choir sang, the director and pianist increased the tempo on whatever hymn the choir was rendering. No matter how slowly it was supposed to be sung, she played faster. Another worshipper played the tambourine as she rocked back and forth.

Toward the end of the service, the minister announced, "While the choir sings, the doors of the church are open. If anyone would like to join the church by letter, faith, or Christian experience, please come forward."

By letter, meant that people could be accepted if they presented a written statement from another church indicating they were Christians and members in good standing.

"Tomorrow is not promised to you. The Bible says that no one knows the day or the hour when the Lord shall return. Won't you come now while you have a chance?"

The first pew at the front of the church was referred to as the Mourner's Bench. If people wanted to establish membership or give their lives to Christ and be baptized, they sat in that pew. That was the time and place to get religion.

One year during The Meeting, as Rebie and I were sitting together, she got up and said to me, "I'm going up there and join the church tonight."

Ruby and Elizabeth, who were older, had joined the church and been baptized a year or two earlier. So, it was time for Rebie and me to become members.

I followed Rebie as I did quite often. We walked to the front and sat in the first pew. After the choir finished the invitational hymn, the minister and the deacons gathered around us and began to sing,

"I will trust in the Lord. I will trust in the Lord.

I will trust in the Lord. Till I die."

"Will you trust Him?" they asked.

Finally, Rebie stood and said she wanted to give her life to Christ. I sat there as if waiting for the Spirit or something to tell me to stand. The minister and the deacons continued to sing,

"Come to Jesus, Come to Jesus. Come to Jesus just now,
Just now, come to Jesus. Come to Jesus just now."

The congregation sang along with the minister and the deacons.

"He will save you. He will save you.
He will save you just now.
Just now he will save you. He will save you just now."

I continued to sit. I wouldn't, just couldn't bring myself to stand. I never moved. The group motioned with outstretched arms for me to stand and accept Christ, but I still didn't budge. They finally said the benediction and ended the service.

"Why didn't you get up?" Mama asked after the service.

"I don't know," I said.

I was really just too bashful to move but agreed to go back the next night.

"When you go up there tomorrow night, stand and let them know that you want to be saved. Just stand and let them know."

The next night, the group didn't have to sing long before I stood and extended my hand to let them know I wanted to become a Christian. I got religion.

Rebie and I were baptized the next Sunday in the church pool. I didn't look forward to the baptismal ceremony because I was afraid of being under water. On that day, everyone who had joined the church during The Meeting was there to be baptized. Reverend Johnson was clad in a long white robe. Rebie and I wore dresses and had our heads covered with towels. As we were led to the pool, the group sang,

"Take me to the water. Take me to the water.

Take me to the water to be baptized."

One of the deacons stood by to assist. Members of the family were in the sanctuary to watch the ceremony. Rebie went first. I followed. The water was cool. After stepping into the pool, we were told to take a deep breath and hold it. Just before being submerged in the water, Reverend Johnson began the Baptismal Ritual.

"I baptize you in the name of the Father and of the Son and the Holy Spirit. Amen."

Shivering as we got out of the water, we rushed to get dressed. Mama was there to help and to let us know how proud she was to have us become Christians.

After becoming a Christian, I tried to do everything right. In Sunday school, we studied the Bible and put emphasis on the Ten Commandments. We were admonished to obey our parents, show love for every one, and treat people the way we wanted to be treated. For the most part, we followed our teachings with a few exceptions. For me, the most embarrassing breach in my training was the time when tempers flared and angry words were exchanged between my cousin and me. We started hitting each other right there in the church. That was a no-no.

After pulling us apart, one of the deacons declared, "You don't act like that in church. Y'all got to go before the congregation and ask to be forgiven."

I had shamed and disgraced my immediate family, as well as my church family. I had already broken my vow to live a Christian life. Embarrassed by what happened and with my head bowed so low that my chin touched my chest, I stood before the congregation the next Sunday with my cousin. Dabbing my eyes to hold back tears, I apologized for what I had done.

I don't remember what the pastor said as we stood there. Confrontations of that type were out of character for me. That taught me a lesson and never again did I get involved in such altercations.

As years passed, all nine girls became members of Cedar Grove Baptist Church and remained active until leaving the area. Today, Ruth is the only one of us who is a member.

Unlike in the 40s, 50s, and 60s, many changes have taken place. The small church has been enlarged. The Meeting is now called The Revival. Services are held more like traditional Baptist churches. The pastor serves only one church, and services are held every Sunday.

Refraining from working on the Sabbath became a thing of the past, too. Regulations called "Blue Laws," which required businesses to be closed on Sunday were repealed. Our understanding of the Bible and the commandments evolved. Much of what ancient writers transcribed and practiced years ago is translated and expressed differently today. I pray that as we go through life if we are violating the principles and teachings of the Bible, the Lord will have mercy and forgive us all.

GREAT-GRANDMA AND UNG GEORGE

Wisdom belongs to the aged
and understanding to the old.
Job 12:12

As we reached our teens, some of us stayed home and cared for our younger sisters while Mama, Daddy, and some of the girls went to town, to church, or to visit relatives. We still had to take turns because all of us couldn't ride comfortably in the car.

Many Saturdays, we visited our great-grandparents, George and Rindy Warren, who lived closer to us at that time than other members of our extended family. We enjoyed visiting them. Great-Grandma took us to pick blueberries that grew in the woods nearby. Mama used the berries to make preserves, which we enjoyed all summer. Bites from chiggers, ticks, and mayflies caused us to itch and scratch for many days but didn't dissuade us from going berry picking. All Great-Grandma had to say was, "It's time to pick berries." We were ready for the trip.

It was evident that Great-Grandma kept lots of stuff. By today's standards, she might be considered a hoarder. She actually kept a piece of Cousin Thelma's wedding cake in a metal trunk for many years. She had lots of old magazines, newspapers, almanacs, calendars, and gadgets. We liked to tinker with the items, which also included old clocks, watches, wind-up toys, rocks, and marbles. Many times, she gave us magazines to read or to use for school projects.

We admired the antique ironstone pitcher and washbasin that she treasured. No one seems to know how she acquired it. We speculated that some of her sons who served in World War II gave it to her or it could have been a gift from some of the farmers for whom she worked. It is kept and cherished as a family heirloom, which will be passed from one generation of our family to another.

While rummaging through her things one day, I discovered a 1941 calendar—my birth year. I was in my teens at the time, which let me know she had kept it for many years. As I quickly flipped to the month of April, my birth month, I learned to my surprise that I was born on Sunday. I had never been told on which day of the week I was born. I thought about poems I had read about Sunday's child.

I didn't tell Great-Grandma about the calendar. I was afraid she wouldn't like my going through her personal items. Mama was surprised when I told her about my discovery. She smiled and looked away as if recalling that day.

"That's right, you certainly were born on Sunday," she said.

When going to visit our great grandparents, we looked forward to seeing the exotic looking bantam chickens, guineas, and the dogs that they raised.

They seemed to have kept the chickens just for pets. With colorful feathers and neatly preened, they strutted or flew around as if to say, "We know we'll never have to worry about our necks being wrung or being dinner for anyone."

Their dogs, of no special breed, were fed ice cream and cookies. Sometimes we wished we could have gotten to their house before the treats were given to the dogs, but we were always a little too late—just in time to see the empty cups and wrappers in the yard.

Pampering their animals was strange behavior for folks in the farming community. We were used to chickens being raised to lay eggs, be eaten, or sold. Dogs were usually fed bones and other scraps from the table.

As years passed and the visits continued, our younger sisters' experiences were different. They saw no exotic chickens, and the dogs didn't seem to get as much attention.

Yvonne and Eileen shared how Great-Grandma usually treated them to delicious bread pudding, baked white sweet potatoes, or pound cake. Ung George shared Johnnycakes with the girls and the dogs. The children, as well as the animals, were served out of the same large cookie jar.

George was Great-Grandma's second husband. We called him Ung George. Most of the locals called him Uncle George. It wasn't uncommon for older men who were well known in the community to be called Uncle. I imagine we weren't taught to call him Great-Grandpa because Robert Vick, Great-Grandma's first husband was our great-grandfather.

Great-Grandma divorced Robert Vick. He was the father of Grandma Esther and the rest of Great-Grandma's children. He continued to live in the area, but we never got to know him.

A missing thumb on Ung George's gnarled arthritic right hand made it difficult for him to do certain chores. We were curious about what happened to it, but for a long time, were too afraid to question him. One day after watching him as he shuffled around trying to complete work in the yard, one of us, I don't know whom, mustered up enough courage and asked, "Ung George, what happened to your thumb?"

"Huh?" he said.

"Why don't you have a thumb on both of your hands?"

After pausing for a moment, he pointed to the house. I remember his saying, "Go ask your great grandma."

Now, Great-Grandma was a feisty lady who didn't talk much, but when she spoke, her shrill voice let you know that she didn't take any mess from anyone. Although some of us were more outgoing than others, no one had enough spunk to ask her about the missing thumb. Whispers among the family hinted that a shot from a gun fired by her resulted in the loss of Ung George's thumb.

We don't know if the rumors were true. Whatever happened, Ung George wasn't willing to tell us. He seemed to confirm the gossip when he sent us to Great-Grandma Rindy for an explanation. We never asked him about his thumb again.

Mama attributed Great-Grandma's combative behavior to her being part Native American. It's possible that she had ties to the Meherrin or Nottoway Indian Tribes that once inhabited the Southampton County area where she lived all of her life. A list of family names of descendants of the Meherrin Tribe includes the last name Scott, which was her mother's maiden name. The 1910 census listed her race as mulatto, an indication that she was more than likely biracial. Her fair complexion was probably considered light skinned when she was younger. With hair that didn't require much straightening—sometimes referred to as "good hair"—she was undoubtedly racially mixed.

What a storyteller Ung George was. He was about eighty years old at that time. The denim bib coveralls and floppy hat he wore made him look just like the old man in *Uncle Remus Stories*. His smooth ebony skin was just the opposite in color of Great-Grandma's. With hair and beard as white as freshly picked cotton, he was quite a character.

On the way to visit them, Daddy sometimes warned us about what to expect from Ung George.

"Well, we gonna stop by George Warren's and listen to him tell some tales now." Sometimes, he said, "We're gonna hear some lies today."

We heard the same stories over and over—how when he was younger, he helped young white couples elope. He explained how he and the young suitors put ladders against the windows of the large two-story farmhouses at night to help the brides-to-be escape—sometimes successfully and sometimes not.

"Me and them boys thought we knowed what to do. One night, we had got the gal 'bout half out the window when her mama saw her. She grabbed her by her long hair and pulled her back. We had to make a fast getaway that night," he said.

He also told how skillful he was at taming horses.

"If I couldn't break 'em, nobody else could," he boasted.

Of course, we had no proof that anything Ung George said was true. He seemed to enjoy an audience and was believed to have fabricated some of his stories just to entertain anyone who listened.

As it got late at night, he sometimes ranted about church folk, the Bible, dying, and his burial. It was evident by then he had been sipping homemade wine or other spirits he was said to brew. He had specific instructions on what was to be done at his death.

"When I die, don't put me in no casket and take me to no church for no funeral. Just put a chain around my neck, get a tractor, drag me to a ditch, and cover me with dirt."

Daddy had a penchant for getting him all riled up and knew exactly what to say to him. "When you die, I'm going to make sure there's a funeral, and you'll be buried right at Mount Carmel Church." That was the church where Great-Grandma's family was buried.

"If you leave this earth before Rindy, I'll make sure there's a plot for her next to you."

Still raving, Ung George continued, "I'm telling you what I want right now. Don't even call the undertaker."

Daddy didn't relent. "Naw, naw, I'm gonna call Johnson's Funeral Home, have them dress you in a suit, put you in a casket, and you won't be able to do anything about it. You know when you're dead, you're done."

"Hubbut, you gon' let folks look at me in a casket? If they can't come to see me while I'm living, I don't want 'em looking at me when I'm dead. What good is looking at me gon' do?"

"Yep, I sure am."

"Okay, okay, jes go 'head," Ung George said as he leaned back pointing his finger. "Go 'head if you want to. You watch and see what's gon' happen. When that casket is opened, I'm gon' jump right up and knock the hell out of you. I mean it. I mean it. I'm gon' knock the hell out of you and anybody that try to look at me."

After high school, I didn't visit our great-grandparents much. Great-Grandma passed in 1961 and Ung George in 1962. Traditional funerals were held for both of them. Although I knew it was impossible, I kept wondering if Ung George would really jump up in his casket when it was time for viewing. Dressed in his moth-eaten black wool suit, he lay as stiff as the boards on the wooden casket in which he was placed. Needless to say, as much as he boasted about what he was going to do, no fistfight occurred between his corpse and the mourners in attendance. He didn't jump up and knock the hell out of anyone.

Elizabeth and Ruby standing by the pecan tree on the Womble farm.

Rebie, age 19, enjoying a hot summer day on the Beale farm.

Me, age 2, beside the
two-room house
where I was born.

Ernell (left) and Minnie
(right) dressed for fun in the
snow.

Eileen on the back porch of the house on the Womble Farm.

Ruth Ann (left) and Yvonne (right) dressed in new Christmas outfits.

Annie Mae Deloatch Harris
(Mama)

Herbert Lee Harris
(Daddy)

Daddy and Mama at Minnie's college graduation.

Daddy and Mama in front of the first home of their own.

Ora Latimer Cox, Daddy's sister,
was a woman of strength whose
support was unwavering.

Aunt Ora, Daddy, and Uncle
Charlie celebrate Aunt Ora's
70th birthday.

Uncle Aurelius Jones,
Daddy's brother, talked
fast and was always
smiling.

Grandma Queen Esther and her sister Pearl (front). Back row
(l to r) Aunt St. Clara, Mama, Uncle Edward, and Aunt Rosa.

Uncle James DeLoatch
(Mama's brother)

Grandma Queen Esther and
Great-Grandma Rindy
holding one of the great-
grandchildren.

Grandma Queen Esther
visited us often on
Sunday after church.

Elizabeth '73   Ruby '57

Rebie '59   Daphne '59   Minnie '61

Ernell '64   Eileen '65   Yvonne '67   Ruth '69

All of us, except Elizabeth and Ruth, graduated from Hayden High
School in Franklin, Virginia. Elizabeth earned a High School
Equivalency Diploma from Norfolk Public Schools. Ruth graduated
from Southwest High School in Nansemond County, Virginia.

Celebrating Aunt Ora's 70th birthday. Front Row (l to r): Eileen, Ruby, Yvonne, and me. Back row: Rebie, Minnie, Ruth, Elizabeth, and Ernell.

The nine of us gathered at Ruth's home after attending Friends and Family Day at church.

(L to R) Ruby, Yvonne, Minnie, Ruth, Rebie, Eileen, Ernell,
and I attend our 2nd annual Thanksgiving Celebration.

During the celebration,
Ruby presented Mama's
onyx and silver necklace
to Rebie.

My family – my husband, James, son-in-law Ivan Bennette, our
daughters Stephanie Bennette and Satonya Dews; and me.

SPARE THE ROD

Direct your children onto the right path,
and when they are older, they will not leave it.
Proverbs 22:6

"Y'all behave yourselves now. Be good while we're gone."

That's what Mama and Daddy always said when they left us at home alone.

"If you don't, you gonna get it when we get back."

Some of us remembered to follow the rules while others misbehaved almost every time.

Having to rear nine girls with different temperaments was not easy. Some of us were more difficult to discipline than others. Most of us were quiet. Some had health issues while others exhibited strong-willed and more aggressive behaviors. Sibling rivalry was so strong among some of us that more often than not, altercations took place whether our parents were at home or not. So, Mama and Daddy didn't spare the rod.

When we were young, scare tactics or a swat on the bottom were enough to get us to behave most of the time. They threatened us with the Boogie Man, Cat Man, and other scary things.

"The Boogie Man is going to come and get you tonight," Daddy said. "He comes and grabs little children that aren't good. You just wait until it gets dark. You better stop what you're doing right now."

At bedtime, all the lights were turned off, and the only light visible on the farm was from the stars and the moon. I got that eerie feeling something was always lurking around outside that would sneak inside and take me away. Not one door could be locked at night, but we still felt safe as long as we were inside.

For me, they knew how scared I was about the death of our horse, Gray Jack. So, for a long time they threatened me with the horse coming back to gallop away with me. If I misbehaved, all they had to say, especially at night, was, "All right Daphne, here comes Gray Jack. I see her looking in the window."

With that, I sat quietly peering at the windowpanes, just waiting for that face and big eyes to appear. When I went to bed, I kept my head under the covers all night. I was scared to peek out and too terrified to get up and use the potty, which resulted in our sleeping in wet beds many nights.

They said the Cat Man would nab naughty children. He will come at night, get you, and scratch your eyes out.

"The Ku Klux Klan will come for you," Daddy also threatened. "They will take you away never to be seen again."

We actually didn't know what the Klan was all about until the 60s during the push for civil rights in the South.

As we got older, scare tactics didn't work. They had to use stronger measures. And boy, oh boy, every technique that someone suggested, our parents must have tried. Being young parents, they consulted older relatives for guidance. Whatever Grandma Esther, Great-Grandma Rindy, Aunt Sally, or Cousin Sarah said they should try, they did. They used the Bible and their interpretation of scriptures as a guide.

Using Time Out, I Messages, Behavior Management Charts with smiley faces, or similar techniques weren't among the suggestions. No one told them about sibling rivalry or behaviors that are common for young children during certain stages of growth and development.

Use of their hands, belts, switches, or sometimes a shoe wasn't uncommon. Punishments that included using an electric extension cord were harsh and left many welts. By today's standards, that would be labeled child abuse, and we would become wards of the state.

Those of us who were strong-willed and most aggressive usually fought each other or got into some type of altercation more often when we were left alone. They required more discipline and were punished more often and most severely.

Our parents weren't aware that those of us with aggressive behaviors were probably attempting to develop independence, just trying to fit into the world around us, or needing guidance and understanding from the two of them. We craved attention, but with so many children, it was apparently not easy to give each child the individual consideration needed.

If we had health problems, we were spared. Ruby shared her reason for their being lenient on her.

"I think they favored me because I had an illness, which was thought to have been Typhoid Fever, when I was very young. I was sick for a long time and not very strong."

Elizabeth, our oldest sister, had seizures, which sometimes occurred during stressful times. She was also mild-mannered. I don't remember her and Ruby ever getting punished.

I cringe when I think of the switches that we had to get from the woods nearby.

"And you might as well get some keen ones," Mama warned as she sent us to get them.

"You don't want me to have to go and get them myself."

We certainly didn't. She knew how to pick switches that would set our little legs on fire. We tried to choose the ones that would be less painful. Seeing them sitting in a corner in the room was enough to make most of us listen and do whatever we were told to do.

Daddy was busy working most of the time, so Mama doled out most of the punishments. Sometimes, we ran so fast that she couldn't catch us. She didn't fret.

"That's all right, I'll just wait until it gets dark," she warned.

She knew well that we feared darkness and when night came, she would know exactly where to find us. We hoped she would forget she was going to spank us, but that was wishful thinking. I looked at her and tried to determine whether or not she had forgotten but could never tell by the expression on her face. I also tried to behave really well, hoping she would not remember. She would be quite pleasant, but right around bedtime, she got those switches. We had nowhere to run and no place to hide.

"I told you that I was going to get you," she said, making a lash with every word. As long as you live in this house, you will have to listen to me and do as I say. Now, go to bed and next time, maybe you'll remember what I told you to do."

With that, we went to bed and whimpered for a while. I was usually more angry than hurt but so glad it was over. Sometimes we got so mad we threatened to report our parents to our teachers but never did.

The few times that Daddy had to intervene are etched in our memories. Just pulling off his belt was enough to make us shape up. Most of us recall being spanked by him at least once. He sometimes said, "I'm going to get you tomorrow."

It was needless to think he would forget, and we don't know why he sometimes chose to wait until the next day. Was he tired from working all day? Or did he just need time to get those horrible switches? We could never figure that one out. When the next day came, he followed through with his promise.

Yvonne shared her agonizing wait and the most memorable reprimand she received from Daddy.

"We were left home alone. While playing, I struck a match and set fire to a string that was hanging from the mantel. It was part of the frayed edges of a scarf that Mama had placed there. The string burned quickly, but we were able to put out the fire before it destroyed the scarf or burned the mantel.

"When Mama and Daddy got home and were told what I had done, I knew I was in trouble. That was severe enough to let Daddy handle the punishment. He let me know that playing with matches was a 'no-no.'"

"'You go on to bed,'" he said. "'Just wait until tomorrow.'"

"The next day, Daddy went to the woods nearby, got fresh switches, and stripped away all of the leaves.

"'Come here,'" he said. "'Now. Don't you remember what I told y'all about playing with matches? I told y'all not to play with matches. You could have set the house on fire.'"

"After that scolding, he gave me a whipping that I haven't forgotten. I didn't dare play with matches again."

When Grandma Queen Esther took care of us, she had a strange way of making us listen to her. She would grasp us by our upper arms, make eye contact, and ask, "Do you want me to shake your frame?"

Her long nose, eagle-like eyes, and furrowed brow were enough to make us too frightened to do anything wrong.

"No, no Grandma," I said. I'll be good. I'll be good."

"Well, you better behave yourself and I mean it," she said.

She shook us violently until we were uncomfortable. I don't remember Grandma actually shaking me, but I knew exactly what she meant. We weren't left with her often, but apparently she kept us long enough for her discipline techniques to be known. Just grabbing my arms and getting my attention usually worked.

During our early teen years, if we were disobedient, we were often grounded, and privileges were taken away. We looked forward to going to town on Saturdays. That was important for us socially. It was the only time we got to see some of our friends, especially during the summer. We wanted to take part in special church and school activities. Permission to attend those functions was often denied and used as consequences for not following rules.

Why did young children have to endure such punishments? One must consider the time and circumstances in which we lived. Our parents were young when they began their family. The first child was born when Mama was 15 and Daddy was 18. The guidance they got from people whom they trusted wasn't necessarily the best child-rearing practices. Religion also played an important part in decisions made during that time—the 40s, 50s, and 60s.

We didn't always understand their methods of punishment and felt that some of them were far too harsh. But we appreciate their trying to provide guidance that enabled us to grow up to be respectful young ladies. I can't imagine what life for us would have been like had we not been given boundaries and consequences for some of our actions.

My sisters and I don't dwell on what we had to endure. The past can't be changed. We know our parents wanted the best for us but just didn't always have the skills and know-how to do what was right and appropriate. For our children, discipline was administered differently. We weren't as young as our parents when we began our families, and none of us had more than three children. We broke the cycle and moved forward.

HAYDEN HIGH SCHOOL

Students are not greater than their teacher.
But the student who is fully trained
will become like the teacher.
Luke 6:40

We made the transition to high school after spending four years in Mrs. Spencer's classroom at Damascus School. Southampton County didn't have a high school for students in the southeastern part of the county. All students in those areas were bused to Franklin City Schools. Negroes went to Hayden High School while whites went to Franklin High School. The districts still didn't have middle-school programs. Elementary school included grades 1-7, and high school was grades 8-11. Grade 12 was added in 1958. The class of '59 was first to complete grade 12. Rebie and I were in that class.

Hayden High School was about five miles away. The bus stop was a mile away because the county still didn't maintain Bumpy Hole Road. Because of that, buses couldn't come to the end of the lane, which led to where we lived.

Ruby was first to attend high school. I remember how proud Mama and Daddy were to finally have a child advance that far. I can still visualize Ruby's brown alligator leather attaché case that Mama purchased for her.

Ruby recalled some of her experiences.

"Getting my gym outfit to wear during P.E. was different than anything that we had experienced at the two-room elementary school. A game of dodge ball was about all we ever had for physical education. I thought I was very skillful at dodging the ball. I remember sticking my tongue out and teasing one of the girls because she couldn't hit me. She aimed the ball and hit me right in my mouth.

"High school was quite different. We had to dress in blue shorts, gold T-shirts—the school colors— and tennis shoes. Games and exercises were well organized, and the shower room was different than anything we had heard of. Being able to take a shower after PE was welcomed.

"That year, the girls wore ballerina skirts with poodles on them. I had one. I don't remember if Mama bought it or if Aunt Ora gave it to me. And I can't forget those black and white saddle shoes that were popular during that time."

Elizabeth, Rebie, and I entered high school a year later. By that time, a new Hayden High School, which was said to be a "separate but equal" replacement for the old school, had been built. "Separate but equal" meant that although the school system was racially segregated, equal facilities were provided for all children. It was a beautiful building with what was considered state-of-the-art equipment.

Several days before school opened, Daddy said, "A new driver is going to be driving the bus this year, and she don't take no mess, so y'all better behave yourselves."

Oh boy, was he right. The first day of school was like taking orders from a drill sergeant when we finally got on the bus. We feared her so much that she didn't have to worry about our causing problems. Being aware that she knew our parents also made a difference.

The driver drove so fast that most mornings she was too early or maybe we were just late. Sometimes she waited for us. If we didn't run, she left us. Having to wait seemed to anger her, and having to run almost a mile made us very tired.

What a totally new experience high school was for us—the first time riding a school bus, the idea of having more than one teacher, and not being confined to the same classroom all day. We were so excited. Meeting new friends and experiencing life beyond Damascus School and the farming community awaited us.

Shiny new lockers for storage of our books and supplies lined the halls. We paid for combination locks to be used on them during the year and returned at the end. It was like entering a whole new world.

A huge library had books that could be checked out, audiovisual materials, and many reference books. The librarian was protective of the area and made sure that we were quiet and orderly. I remember spending many of my study periods there with a group of friends talking to Willie, a student from Africa, as he discussed life in his country. He had been sponsored or adopted by a family who lived in the county.

An aroma-filled lunchroom awaited the students. We rarely had money to buy lunch. Sometimes we took sandwiches or just went without lunch. The latter was usually the norm. With so many of us in school at the same time, it was impossible for our parents to provide money for lunch. Unlike today, no programs assisted with meals for needy children.

Elizabeth, Rebie, and I were placed in the same homeroom. I could never understand that decision since the school had two eighth grade classes. Elizabeth was oldest, but health problems had caused her to miss many days of school and repeat grades. No summer programs were held where students could make up classes.

We benefitted greatly from the Home Economics Department with its fancy new ranges and sewing machines. Mrs. Turner, a compassionate teacher, taught skills that continue to impact our lives—how to construct garments, how to set a table, and how to prepare meals. She also taught us a unique way to make beds using tailored tucks, a technique that many of us continue to use today.

Social skills included table manners. "Sit erectly. No elbows on the table. Chew your food with your mouths closed," she instructed.

Learning to use the sewing machine was easy for us. We had an old treadle machine at home and already had experiences using patterns and sewing. So, making an apron, which was a class requirement, wasn't a complicated task.

"I learned to sew so well that Mrs. Turner asked me to make a pair of culottes for her," Ernell recalled. I also made a jumper, which she asked me to model. I strutted so proudly that my classmates said they thought I was going to plunge off the stage."

Minnie seems to have enjoyed Mrs. Turner's instructions so much that she chose that field when she went to college. She continues to benefit from skills learned in the class.

Most of us older girls were placed in general curricula when entering high school. Choosing certain classes wasn't an option. Wherever we were placed, we followed that schedule and performed as best we could. I still don't understand why I never took a foreign language when all of my sisters were afforded that opportunity.

We missed many days of school because of farm chores. Living so far from the highway was an advantage for us at that time. It spared us the embarrassment of having our classmates see us in the fields working as they rode the bus to school. Had they been able to see us, they probably would have teased us. If we weren't at the bus stop, no one knew why, and no one questioned us when we returned to school. None of us wanted to miss school, not one day. Daddy just couldn't do all of the work and didn't have money to hire help.

We also missed many days because of inclement weather. Bad weather affected conditions on the dirt road, which sometimes made it difficult for Daddy to take us to school or to the bus stop. In elementary school, I actually sat by the window on some of those days and chanted, "Rain, rain, go away. Come again another day."

We enjoyed school and learning. We all had dreams and aspirations. I imagine the teachers figured we were unlikely to accomplish very much because of our sporadic attendance or that it would be a miracle if we attended long enough to graduate.

Attendance for my younger sisters improved greatly. They didn't have to help on the farm much. Opportunities for them were different.

Someone once asked, "How did you get an education while having to endure such hardships?" I was really caught off guard and didn't know how to answer that question. Days later, I listened as an accomplished songwriter who had fallen on hard times and lived on the streets for a long time answered a similar question. His response was, "Just because you're poor doesn't mean that you are stupid or can't learn, and being deprived doesn't define who you are and what you can achieve in life." He said just what I would have liked for my answer to have been.

As we advanced from grade to grade and became more involved in school activities despite the odds, most of us did fairly well. Ernell and I sang in the school choir. Rebie was a member of Future Business Leaders of America (FBLA).

I remember one year when the standardized test results were received, my homeroom teacher praised some of the students who had done well. My name was included in her comments. That really boosted my self-esteem and encouraged me to work harder.

Yvonne recalled her experiences.

"When I was in high school, I was selected class president during my senior year. Delivering a speech at commencement was one of my proudest moments. I also played the trumpet in the band, sang in the school choir, and was a member of FBLA."

As most of us graduated from high school, we made plans to leave the area. Elizabeth actually left before completing Hayden and found employment in Norfolk, VA.

Graduation day was a special time for each of us, as well as the family. Aunt Ora, Aunt Saint Clara, and other relatives usually attended the ceremonies and beamed with pride. If we needed white dresses for that day, we could always depend on Aunt Ora to make them. Graduation dresses were the last that she made for each of us. The last white dress that she purchased was Ruby's wedding dress.

Every one or two years, one of us was in the graduating class at Hayden High School. Ruby graduated in 1957 and went to live in Norfolk. Rebie and I finished in 1959 and went to live in Washington, DC. A year later, I entered college. Minnie was in the class of '61, Ernell in '64, and Eileen in '65. Minnie went to Norfolk Division of Virginia State College, now Norfolk State University. Ernell went to live in New York. Eileen joined the Job Corps and went to a center in Maine. Yvonne would be last to graduate from Hayden High School.

In 1966, Southampton County finally consolidated all schools for Negro children. That involved many changes and improved educational experiences, but the schools didn't integrate.

The United States Supreme Court had ruled in 1954 that segregated schools were unlawful. The State of Virginia, determined to avoid implementing the law, adopted Massive Resistance. That policy, which was designed to block desegregation of public schools, lasted in many rural districts until the early 1970s. Some systems closed schools rather than desegregate. Many areas established or expanded private academies.

Damascus Elementary School was closed as consolidation took place. The children were reassigned to Jerusalem District Elementary School and Riverview High School in Courtland, VA, more than ten miles away. Ruth was the only one of us attending school in the county at that time. Yvonne continued to go to Hayden High School in the city of Franklin since that was her last year. Transportation to and from school had to be arranged by our parents. One of the teachers who lived in the area agreed to take Yvonne to school.

Ruth no longer had to walk a mile to the bus stop. The county began to maintain Bumpy Hole Road. Having the county control the upkeep of the road was a godsend. It made conditions so much easier for driving to the highway. A school bus stop was located at the end of the lane that led to where we lived.

Ruth shared her excitement about the changes.

"It was great not having to take that long walk to the highway to get the bus. With a new stop, I usually stood on the front porch until I saw the bus coming. I could run to the stop by the time the bus got there and turned around.

"I was assigned to Jerusalem District Elementary School, which was larger, and unlike Damascus, had many rooms. Mrs. Spencer was also assigned to that school, but I wasn't in her classroom. I had several teachers, which included resource teachers for music and physical education. There was an area, which served as a lunchroom and auditorium where hot meals were served. I no longer took lunch to school."

The educational opportunities my older sisters and I experienced and those for our younger sisters were quite different. It's unfortunate that all of us didn't have the same privileges. Getting to and from school would certainly have been easier for us. We could have avoided missing school because it was too cold or rainy for us to walk to the highway, or the road was so obstructed with mud holes that Daddy couldn't drive his car through them to take us to school.

Sometimes change is a long time coming. It seems to have taken forever in the rural area where we lived.

TEENAGERS AND DATING

Give me understanding and I will obey your instructions.
I will put them into practice with all my heart.
Psalm 119:34

Life for us changed tremendously when we became teenagers. The family got its first television, which helped to expose us to a whole new world of knowledge and experiences. The entire family enjoyed *The Ed Sullivan Show, Gunsmoke, I Love Lucy, The Lone Ranger, Amos and Andy, The Little Rascals,* and *Leave It to Beaver.* Watching the news with commentators like Edward R Murrow, Douglas Edwards, and Walter Cronkite kept us informed of events occurring around the world.

Dick Clark's *American Bandstand* was our favorite. Watching that show helped us learn the latest rock and roll hits and the latest dances. We knew the names of all of the dancers in the show. We became aware of fashion trends and what life was like for teenagers in large cities.

The "soaps" were also popular. We rushed home daily to see what was happening on *The Guiding Light, Search for Tomorrow,* and *As The World Turns.*

It was important that we kept up with the latest styles and trends. Skirts with heavily starched crinoline slips were a must have. If we didn't have starch, we used a mixture of flour and water to stiffen the slips. In winter, wool skirts with what we called "kick pleats" in the back were worn. Cardigan or crew-neck sweaters and blouses were popular. Knee-high socks were worn in winter and "bobby socks" during warm weather. We didn't have many choices for shoes. Most teens had black and white saddle shoes or flats.

We straightened our hair with combs and curling irons, which were heated on the hot stove. Styles were usually bangs with braids or curls. Hair was sometimes rolled at night. If we didn't have hair rollers, we improvised by using twisted strips of paper from brown paper bags to make rollers. Girls with long hair wore curls or ponytails. Young people didn't wear wigs or hairpieces.

For church, young girls could wear heels and silk stockings. Really great shoes could be purchased for $3 to $4 per pair—usually black for winter and white for summer. We didn't dare go to church without stockings.

Transistor radios, record players, and teen magazines sparked our interest as we tried to involve ourselves in activities like the young people that we saw at school each day. With transistor radios, we listened to local radio stations while doing chores. During our spare time, it was fun reading teen and romance magazines.

Our parents were still quite young, so they liked listening to recordings played on the record player. From time to time, they purchased the latest rock-and-roll records for us.

Ebony and *Jet* magazines and the *Norfolk Journal and Guide* newspaper kept us informed of activities involving Negroes across the nation. Local newspapers and major magazines didn't print much news about Blacks.

Pictures of Emmit Till, who was brutally slain in Mississippi, were in some of our first issues of *Jet*. Those images are forever etched in our memories.

Our teen years actually coincided with the great societal changes of the 50s and 60s. A push for racial equality, especially in the South led by Dr. Martin Luther King Jr. and many civil rights advocates, captured the nation's attention. The Vietnam War was raging. There was a cold war between the United States and the Soviet Union. Much unrest and protesting took place in the large cities of our country. Just as we were going through all of the changes associated with being teenagers, our country and the world experienced great changes, too.

As time passed, some of us began to get interested in guys and dating—or should I say, they began to pay attention to us. That didn't happen easily. Growing up with only girls made us bashful and reluctant to talk to boys or date. We just weren't accustomed to mingling with members of the opposite sex.

Sometimes Daddy took us to the Teenage Club in Franklin on weekends. It was owned and operated by none other than Mrs. Spencer, our elementary school teacher. Mama and Daddy didn't mind our going to the club. They probably felt that with Mrs. Spencer in charge, we would be safe.

I imagine our teacher was continuing to try to make an impact on our social development. There, we could interact with young people our age. When dancing, couples were reminded to show respect.

"Don't dance too close together," she insisted. "Boys should approach the girls and ask, 'May I have this dance?'"

For me, being there was awkward. I was never much of a dancer.

Several of us never dated while we lived at home. Eileen revealed her experiences. "I never dated until I graduated from high school and moved away from home. At school, the guys kept asking me, 'Eileen, are you a virgin? Eileen, are you a virgin?' Mama and Daddy had never told us about the birds and the bees. So, at that time, I didn't know what they were talking about."

Most of us who dated were never allowed to go out with guys alone. We had to double date, which Rebie and I did. We went to dances, to church, and to the senior prom together. We had to be home by 11. If guys visited, they had to leave by that time. Eleven o'clock was what Daddy called "Get Your Hat Time." A clock was on the mantel in the living room, and Mama and Daddy had one in their bedroom. While they sat in their room, they could probably hear every word that was said. If it got too quiet, Daddy actually went outside and peered though the window to make sure that nothing out of the ordinary was going on. He never let anyone know what he was up to until one night it was raining and he came in soaking wet. He realized he had let the cat out of the bag because we realized what he was doing.

"When the clock struck eleven, we didn't chance letting our guest stay any longer," Rebie explained. "If we chose not to follow the rules, the door was opened and Daddy said, 'Y'all boys don't know what time it is, do you? It's past eleven. So, it's time for y'all to go home.' With that scolding, the guys left immediately. We were quite embarrassed, but rules had to be followed."

During the summer with so many chores to do, we didn't have much time for dating, except on Saturday afternoon or Sunday. Sometimes, guys stopped by during the week or on Saturday and discovered we were in the fields working. They were kind enough to wait until we finished our chores. If Daddy didn't particularly trust them, it was a different story.

Once, two friends stopped by while we were busy and were quickly turned away. For years, we didn't even know that they had come to visit. Later, we found out that as soon as they got there, Daddy said, "Y'all boys might as well go home. These girls have work to do. They don't have time to talk."

Without telephones, they had no way of getting permission to visit prior to their coming. It was not uncommon for friends to stop by without our knowing they were planning to visit.

The guys had walked quite a distance, but they knew when Daddy spoke, he meant just what he said, and they had to leave. It was evident that Daddy didn't think too highly of them.

The younger sisters didn't have to endure rules that were quite so strict. Mama and Daddy were more lenient with them.

"Even if Daddy didn't like the guys I dated, they were allowed to visit," Yvonne said. "He was still reluctant to let me go out with them alone. I might have gone out alone at least once."

When people learn we had nine girls in our family, one of the first questions asked is: how did your father manage being in a household with ten females? Daddy didn't appear to have difficulty with all of us being the same sex, even as teenagers. We never heard him express any negative feeling about being the only male in the house or that he would like to have had boys. I imagine at times when he had so much work to do on the farms, he probably wished for males to help with some of the chores.

With so much to be done on the farm, Daddy was busy most of the time. When he had time to spare, he played with us or just engaged in conversation. He was a fun guy and seemed to like telling stories that made us laugh. He also liked to tease us about guys whom he thought were interested in us. I imagine he and Mama were happy for those teen years to end.

ON THE MOVE AGAIN – THE BELKOV FARM

Faith is the confidence that what we hope for will
actually happen. It gives us assurance about things we
cannot see.
Hebrews 11:1

As major changes took place in the schools, life on the farm became stressful for the family. Daddy had problems with the landowner. I don't know everything that happened, but it was evident that communication and cooperation between the two of them had deteriorated to the point where it was time to think about leaving the Beale farm.

"I'm gonna buy me a piece of land and build me a house," Daddy vowed every time they had disagreements.

"The man wants me to let him buy my peanuts for seed for next year's planting. But he don't want to pay me as much as I can get by selling them on the open market. That's not right. I can make more money if I sell them myself."

It was impossible for Daddy to purchase land and have a house built. His farming just didn't generate enough income. When profits were shared with the owner, little was left for the family.

Continuing to be at odds with the landowner, he began searching for another farm. In fact, it was agreed that the family would move at the end of the year in 1966.

This time, Daddy wanted to lease acreage. Finding land wasn't easy. With modern machines, farmers were able to cultivate many acres. That made small farms hard to find.

By the end of the year, after searching here and there, Daddy located a farm in Nansemond County. As luck would have it, Ruby's husband, James, was employed by the wholesale distributing company, which owned the farm. Daddy contacted the owners and expressed his desire to lease the farm. As soon as an agreement was complete, he announced, "Y'all get everything packed. We have to be off this farm by the end of December."

It had been eight years since I finished high school and moved away from the Beale Farm. That's the last farm on which I lived. A new community and another farm awaited the rest of the family. For the first time, they would no longer live in Southampton County.

In January 1967, the family moved to the Belkov farm in Nansemond County, which was about 15 miles away. Located along a paved road, it wasn't nearly as isolated as areas where the family had lived before. We could actually sit on the porch and watch traffic go by. Unlike the Beale farm, where the mailbox was a mile away and we couldn't see the highway, Mama could sit on the porch and watch the mail carrier deliver the mail. She could also watch Ruth, the youngest sister, get the bus to school.

The white frame house had four rooms—two bedrooms, a living room, and a kitchen. A magnolia tree provided shade in the front yard just as the oak tree on the Beale farm. They still had no indoor plumbing or bathroom. They continued to use an outhouse and draw water from a pump in the yard.

For the first time, the family was able to get telephone service. Only party lines were available. Several families used the same telephone line. Each family on the line had a different ring tone. When the phone rang, each household could tell when it should answer.

"I don't like that kind of telephone," Mama complained. "Sometimes when the phone rings, the neighbors pick up the phone and listen to our conversations. If we want to make a call, we have to wait until they finish talking. They even interrupt us and say mean things when we're talking, especially if they think we're spending too much time on the line."

Because of the telephone service and other issues, I don't think Mama and Daddy bonded well with the neighbors. They had lived in areas where even though they were somewhat isolated, folks got along. The next six years weren't the best for them, but they had gone through tough times before.

All of us, except Yvonne and Ruth, had moved away. Having only two girls living at home made conditions in the small house much more comfortable.

Yvonne was in her senior year at Hayden High School and served as president of the class. With plans made for graduation in June, she wanted to continue to attend the school until the end of the school year. Since she was not living in the Franklin City School District, our parents had to get special permission and make arrangements for transportation. Her graduation was symbolic for us, since she would be the last one of us to graduate from Hayden High School. Her picture would grace the hall of the school among the enlarged group photos of many of the graduating classes. After graduation, she went to work at the Naval Air Station in Norfolk and attended Norfolk State College, now Norfolk State University.

Ruth transferred to Southwestern High in Nansemond County and graduated in 1969. Mama and Daddy would soon have an empty nest. After graduation, Ruth married, and her family purchased a home nearby.

For the first time in many years, except for the grandchildren spending time with them during the summer, Mama and Daddy lived in a home without children. Daddy continued to plant corn, cotton, peanuts, and soybeans. He purchased better farm machinery, which enabled him to do most of the work himself. Mama's job was taking care of the home and garden or helping Daddy whenever she was needed.

Having an empty nest didn't stop them from planting a large garden that included tomatoes, cabbage, green peas, butterbeans, sweet potatoes, white potatoes, and a variety of leafy greens, collards, and corn. Mama continued to freeze most of what was grown and share with us when we visited. It was always good to go home and get homegrown vegetables.

The acreage on the farm was small, but more land was leased nearby. Hogs were raised in great numbers. Sometimes Daddy had so many that I don't think he knew the exact count. By that time, the hogs were mostly sold to support the two of them. Economic conditions improved.

The farm had no smoke house or chicken coop. I don't remember hogs being slaughtered or the family having chickens. Since the nine of us were grown and gone, they didn't need lots of chickens. With supermarkets in the area, it was easier for the two of them to shop for groceries in Franklin or Suffolk.

About three years passed and as both parents approached middle age, they began to experience health problems. Each developed hypertension and diabetes. Daddy kept having excruciating pain in his legs while walking. After a visit to a doctor, he was diagnosed with the beginning stages of cardiovascular disease. The prognosis wasn't good. A femoral artery bypass had to be done. For many weeks, he couldn't do the farm chores. His sons-in-law and grandsons had to take care of the livestock and perform other chores.

After Daddy recovered from surgery, we began to hear him repeat that vow made year after year to "buy me a piece of land and build me a house." It was evident that he was beginning to realize that he would soon have to stop farming.

This time it was different. He was serious about his plans. He had heard that the Farmers Home Administration (FHA) and the United States Department of Agriculture (USDA) were making special efforts to improve housing in rural areas. Residents who owned or could secure land were encouraged to take part in the attempts to improve housing in the region. He knew families that were involved in the program.

Daddy set out to find that piece of land. After searching for months, he came home one day with good news to share with Mama.

"I have found some land," he said. "I just have to figure out how to pay for it."

"And where did you find it?" she asked.

He had found a lot for sale in the neighboring county and had gone as far as talking to the landowner about purchasing it.

"It's in Isle of Wight County—just across the Blackwater River—close to the Southampton County line."

How to purchase the land was the next ordeal that he had to contend with. He still didn't have enough income from the farm to secure it. After our parents had a long talk with the nine of us, those who could contribute financially pooled our funds and assisted Mama and Daddy in purchasing the property. It wasn't easy for us, but we felt that our parents had sacrificed so much for us; it was imperative that they have our support. They were quite pleased with our decision. The whole family rejoiced. For the first time, they would be landowners.

Everyone looked forward to the time when a house could be built. Daddy didn't waste any time planning to make his vow come true. That would be the end of the family's moving from one farm to another.

A Home of Our Own

My people will live in safety, quietly at home.
Isaiah 32:18

We talked to Daddy as he made plans for us to see the lot he had purchased.

"If y'all come home on Saturday, I can take you to see it," he promised.

We visited the site with excitement and anticipation. Located along a paved road, later named Wood Duck Drive, it was a great place for a home. It had once been farmland where peanuts and corn were grown. Maple, oak, and pine seedlings dotted the landscape as if waiting for a house to be built to complete the picture. We dug some of the pine seedlings to take back with us to plant on our lawns.

Most important, residents of the small community were friends and neighbors that Mama and Daddy had known for a long time. Many of them were members of Cedar Grove Baptist Church. What a godsend!

The next challenge was to figure out how to pay for having a house built on the property. Where would they get the money? They still didn't have enough income from the farm to support such a venture. The nine of us could offer only moral support. We were just beginning careers and families of our own.

The FHA and USDA were continuing to promote the development of affordable housing in rural areas. Daddy applied for the program and was accepted. Through those agencies, residents were assisted with getting building contractors, financing, and planning in the construction of housing.

"But we still have to figure out how to pay for a house," Mama said. "You can't keep trying to farm and pay for a house, too."

"I know," Daddy replied. "I'm just going to give up farming and find a job somewhere."

At that time because of recurrent health issues, Daddy had already decided he wouldn't be able to continue working the way he had all his adult life. Caring for the livestock, operating the machinery, and performing all of the additional duties on the farm had become too much for him. When work on the farm was not so demanding, he took part-time jobs wherever work was available. He probably had some knowledge of what type of job he could get. He was in his late 50s, so age was a factor.

Applications were filed at many places as he looked for employment. Determined to have that house built, he had already secured a builder based on his income from the farm. Since he had no job, no intentions to continue farming, and a builder ready to start, we wondered what he was going to do. What we didn't know was that the builder had offered him a job until he could find work elsewhere. He was looking for something permanent.

Shortly before beginning work with the builder, Daddy got an offer he said was the best job he'd ever had. Virginia Department of Transportation (VDOT) hired him. The family was elated. No more work on the farm and a new home would soon be built. What a triumphant time for all of us. Daddy couldn't wait to report for work.

Being assigned to work in the Western District of Southampton County pleased him. He had lived in the county most of his life and was familiar with all the districts.

"Shucks, I know that area like the back of my hand," he said. "I know where all the roads are located."

His job wasn't difficult, and his medical conditions didn't affect his performance. He cared for the new truck he was issued just like he owned it and didn't want it used by other employees.

"I don't want nobody driving my truck," he grumbled. "They drive too fast and don't keep it clean."

One day while directing traffic as work crews repaired the highway, he was pleasantly surprised when he stopped an impressive looking car with New Jersey license plates. As the distinguished looking gentleman behind the wheel rolled down the window he asked, "Is that you Herbert?"

To Daddy's surprise, it was his half-brother, whom he had not seen for a long time. He still lived in New Jersey but was on his way to Florida. After a short chat, Uncle Aurelious continued his trip but promised to stop for a visit when driving back through the area.

Each day as Daddy continued to go to work, the builder was busy with the soon-to-be new house. A three-bedroom ranch model was selected.

"Since it's just the two of us now, a small house will be just fine," Mama said.

Colors, kitchen cabinets, bathroom fixtures, carpeting, and other choices had been made. We didn't like the carpeting that was selected for the living room. The colors and designs weren't what we thought were appropriate. Being strong-willed, Mama declared, "I picked the carpeting I wanted."

We knew right away that when Mama made a decision, it would be hard for us to get her to change her mind. After all, she was entitled to have her home just the way she wanted it.

Daddy stopped by the building site often on his way home from work to check on the builder's progress. On weekends, he took Mama to see it.

It didn't take long for the home to be completed. Daddy had already begun to get rid of most of the farm equipment he owned. Several pieces would be taken to the new place to be used for gardening.

When the home was finished, plans were made for what would be the last move that our parents would make—moves that had taken them from farm to farm and situations where they had to deal with the demands of one landowner after another. They were about to take ownership of property that they could finally call their own.

On moving day, Mama and Daddy beamed with pride. I can only imagine how happy they were. Daddy's career as a farmer had come to an end.

The new home was just perfect for them—modest but a far cry from anywhere they had lived before. Along with the three bedrooms, it had a kitchen and open dining area, and living room. For the first time, they would live in a house with indoor plumbing and a bathroom. Being able to have hot and cold water in the house was something we had looked forward to for a long time. We were also pleased that we no longer had to use an outhouse.

Decorating the house was the combined effort of Mama and the nine of us. We purchased items we thought Mama needed and would like. Towels for the bathroom, curtains for the kitchen, bed linens, and pictures for the walls helped to beautify the home. Some of us bought flowers and planted them in the yard.

Mama continued to enjoy gardening. Her pride and joy were the most beautiful yellow chrysanthemums that grew year after year in front of the house. Azaleas in spring, crepe myrtles in summer, and mums in fall provided a beautiful view, which was admired by the whole family, as well as passers-by.

A tire from the tractor was a centerpiece for the backyard. Although it was filled with flowers, it was a reminder of time spent on the farms.

Just as always, Daddy planted a large vegetable garden. For a while, he raised pigs. That venture didn't last long because he didn't have enough space. Hogs also attracted too many flies and had a most unpleasant odor. I imagine the neighbors were quite happy when that attempt ended.

The spacious backyard was ideal for family gatherings and reunions. On most holidays, the nine of us and our families gathered to celebrate with our parents. The grandchildren had plenty of space to romp and play. By that time, they had several. The first three were boys. That all-girls cycle had finally been broken.

Having a place of their own was a great change for Mama and Daddy. She was happy taking care of the home, and he was content with his job. He continued to work for VDOT until he retired at 65.

Daddy's adjustment to retirement wasn't easy. After a few months, he was tired of spending so much time at home and not having a great deal to occupy his time.

"I just can't sit around here all day," he said. "I have to find me something to do. I'm going to look for a part-time job."

So, off he went to a local supermarket and got a job as a bagger. He enjoyed seeing and chatting with the shoppers. One day someone looked at him and said, "You are the oldest bagboy I have ever seen." That didn't deter him. He worked two or three days each week.

Later, he worked part-time for a meat packing company. I think he enjoyed working there because his longtime friend and neighbor worked there.

Unfortunately, both parents continued to have health problems, which got worse each year. Pretty soon, Daddy had to completely stop working and spend more time with Mama. He resigned himself to working in the garden and taking care of the lawn. He also helped with preparing meals. He became a fairly good cook. His specialty was making old-fashioned sweet potato puddings that tasted just like the ones Mama made.

Their health didn't stop them from hosting family gatherings and reunions. They also continued to enjoy having a home of their own.

"This home is the only property we have owned. All of us have worked hard to get it and keep it. I want to always keep it in the family," Mama admonished us.

So far, the property is owned by all of us and is rented. We are determined to honor our parents' wishes and keep ownership of the property in the family as long as possible.

THE CHAIN IS BROKEN

Our hearts are sick and weary
and our eyes grow dim with tears.
Job 16:16

The telephone rang at about seven o'clock that Saturday morning. As soon as I heard Daddy's voice, I panicked and sensed that what he was about to say wasn't good news.

"Something has happened to Annie Mae. I can't get her to respond when I try to wake her," he said.

"Call the rescue squad," I demanded as he described her condition.

"I don't think there's a need for that," he said. "I think she's already gone."

"Well call anyway," I insisted.

As Daddy hung up the phone, I also thought she was probably gone but felt that having the rescue squad there would mean that Daddy wouldn't be alone until some of us could get there. The coroner could also be notified if she had expired.

Daddy had already called Ruth, who lived in Franklin, which wasn't far away. She was on her way.

Crying and getting dressed at the same time, I told James, Satonya, and Stephanie that Daddy needed us right away. In a few minutes, we were on our way to Zuni. The drive from Virginia Beach would take about 55 minutes.

It had been just two days since I visited Mama. I drove out there on Thursday, picked her up, and took her to Portsmouth to visit Aunt Rebecca, who was recuperating at home after being hospitalized. It was a wonderful visit. When I took her home, I felt comfortable leaving her. As we said our goodbyes, she appeared to have been feeling well. I had no idea I might be seeing her alive for the last time that Thursday.

The drive to Zuni didn't take long. Since it was early Saturday morning, traffic wasn't bad. I kept trying to be strong for my girls. When we got to Wood Duck Drive, I saw that the rescue squad's vehicle was still in front of the house. My worst fears were about to become reality. "She must really be gone," I cried.

As I got out of the car and walked slowly up the steps, Daddy, Ruth, and a member of the squad met me.

"I'm very sorry," the attendant said. "She's gone."

"May I see her?" I asked.

With that, I was led to her room. Sometime during the night, she had passed away. I can only hope it was a peaceful transition.

Distraught, I cried for a long time but had to try to work through some of my grief in order to support Daddy and notify my sisters.

Ruby and her husband, James, arrived shortly. They were getting ready for a weekend trip to North Carolina when Daddy called. They also drove from Virginia Beach. Six more girls needed to be contacted.

"Let me call them," my brother-in-law, James insisted.

I remember he'd just gotten a new cell phone and wanted to spare us of all the screams and cries that were heard from my sisters as they learned of Mama's death. While we sat quietly inside, he sat in his truck and broke the news to the rest of the girls. In a short while, everyone was notified—Elizabeth in Norfolk, Rebie in Maryland, Minnie and Ernell in New York, Eileen in Boston, and Yvonne in Atlanta. All of them planned to travel to Zuni as soon as possible.

Mama's health had begun to decline eleven years earlier. She collapsed at church one Saturday while decorating the dining area with mums, which were cut from those growing in her front yard. Daddy rushed her to the hospital in Franklin. Her condition was serious, so she was airlifted from Southampton Memorial Hospital in Franklin to Norfolk General Hospital in Norfolk. She had suffered a massive stroke, which left her with paralysis in her left hand and her speech slightly slurred. Four or five days later, her condition became critical. At that time, she wasn't expected to live through the night.

"If she lives, her condition will be vegetative," the doctor warned.

Based on their findings, the doctors suggested that the family have all life support removed. We met and reluctantly decided to let her go peacefully.

Every sister, cousin, aunt, uncle, and other family member in the area came to the hospital that night. A vigil in and around her room lasted until after midnight—long after hospital visiting hours had ended. Cousin Linward prayed for a long time. As he and most of the family left the room, he said, "She's going to be all right. Everything is in God's hands."

The hospital staff did something that night that I hadn't experienced. As the group of us waited quietly near the room, a serving cart with various types of soft drinks and water was provided for us. Their kindness was appreciated and never forgotten.

Since Elizabeth had nursing experience, she spent the night with Mama. Early the next morning, she was quite surprised when Mama awakened and asked for something to eat. The doctor was summoned.

"All I have to say is, someone must have really prayed last night," he declared while visiting Mama that morning. Surprised at her condition, he ordered treatments to resume right away.

Her recovery was unlike what the doctors had predicted. After several days, she was discharged from the hospital. Her sister, Aunt Saint Clara, spent many weeks caring for her. Being strong-willed, Mama was determined to take care of herself. After many months, her health improved. She continued to do chores around the house, as well as take care of her flowers. We visited on weekends and helped with the most difficult tasks. Over the next eleven years from time to time, she suffered mini strokes, which weakened her and finally caused her death.

It didn't take long for the funeral home to have someone come to pick up Mama's body. All of us gathered in the living room as it was taken away. I don't think any of us could bear seeing her remains taken out of the house. It was so hard letting her go. With a funeral to plan and many relatives to contact, we had to pull ourselves together even though we were distraught and our hearts were broken. We also had to be strong for Daddy.

Seven days later, funeral services were held at Cedar Grove Baptist Church, which was filled to capacity with family, friends, and coworkers. The funeral director was careful when getting the nine of us in the procession. She made sure that the first daughter, Elizabeth, walked beside Daddy. "Where is daughter number two?" she whispered. "And number three?" she asked, as she made sure that we were positioned in the order of our birth. Before that day, it had been awhile since all of us had attended church together.

More floral arrangements than I'd imagined filled the little church. If I had to assist in planning the funeral again, I would certainly suggest charitable donations in lieu of flowers although we really did appreciate the many expressions of sympathy.

After the ceremony, Mama was laid to rest next to her sister Saint Clara at Beulahland Cemetery.

In the days and weeks after the funeral, we tried to adjust to Mama's death.

"I haven't had a good day since your mama passed," Daddy said to me one day as I visited him.

It was evident that he missed her very much. As his health continued to fail, we had to decide whether he should live alone or with one of us. By that time, he had suffered kidney failure, was taking dialysis treatments three times per week, and needed the services of health-care assistants.

"I'm going to stay right here in my house," he insisted when we talked to him about his living arrangements.

Each of us took time off from our jobs to take care of him. Elizabeth spent six weeks with him.

After a few months, his bout with cardiovascular disease required him to have more surgeries on the veins in his legs. As the disease progressed over the next year, one leg was amputated. While spending months in rehabilitation, he began to have problems that led to amputation of the second leg.

Daddy was always active and quite jovial. The day of his second amputation, I could sense that he wouldn't be with us much longer. Having to deal with being a double amputee and taking dialysis three times a week just seemed too much for him to endure. I don't feel he wanted to exist that way.

After the surgery when he was placed in a room, we took turns visiting him. We could tell he was slipping away. Seemingly, he kept his eyes open long enough to see all his daughters who had rushed to his bedside. Minnie and Ernell, who drove from New York, were the last to get there. After their visit with him, his last words to us as we left his room were, "Y'all take care of yourselves, now."

Early the next morning, we got a call indicating that Daddy's condition was grave, and we needed to consider removing life support. Before we could get to the hospital, he passed. We never thought that just 14 months after Mama's death, we would have to face the loss of our father. Following his funeral, he was placed to rest beside Mama in Beulahland Cemetery, Southampton County. After being married more than 57 years, their earthly journey ended, and they are together forever.

THE ONYX AND SILVER NECKLACE

And all who had silver and bronze objects
gave them as a sacred offering to the Lord.
Exodus 35:23

The next several months were spent deciding what to do with our parents' belongings. That was not an easy task although the estate was small.

After Mama's death, we attempted to talk to Daddy about her personal items. We were surprised at his response.

"Don't move anything," he said. "Just leave everything the way Annie Mae left them."

Not wanting to make life stressful for him, we honored his wishes and let Mama's things remain as she left them until after he passed 14 months later.

Among the items Mama left that have impacted the family most are sterling silver and onyx beads, which were once a necklace.

During the holiday season, we usually gave Mama and Daddy monetary gifts—cash that could be used to buy special items after the holidays. Mama saved the money and often stashed it inside our old upright piano.

"Open the top of the piano," she said to me one day while I was spending time with her. "Look to the right and you will see my wallet. That's my secret hiding place."

She had placed the wallet on a ledge where she could easily get it. Sometimes, she let me take the money and deposit it in the bank.

After the holidays, she went to town to shop. She especially liked going to the local jewelry store. By that time, prices had been reduced, and there wasn't the hustle and bustle of so many people trying to shop. On one of her many trips to the store, she purchased a beautiful onyx and sterling silver-beaded necklace. It was a perfect match for many of the clothes she wore. It also complemented her silver-gray hair as she aged gracefully.

From time to time, the cord in the necklace became frayed and broke. Mama used a needle and thread to put the strand back together. As she aged and became ill, it wasn't always easy for her to restring the beads. Paralysis in her hands, which resulted from her having a series of strokes, made it difficult for her to perform tedious tasks. She usually kept the beads in a Mason jar until she felt up to restringing them. Some of them were lost before they could be put back together. In spite of all the difficulties encountered, she managed to keep most of them.

After her death, the beads were discovered. Gone was the silver clasp that held them together. The silver beads were tarnished and had lost the luster and sparkle they once had. The onyx beads were marred of their original natural beauty. They needed to be polished and restrung into the beautiful necklace Mama always cherished. Each time attempts were made to restring the beads, it was difficult to form the patterns the way Mama had always done.

To preserve their memories and continue traditions our parents started long ago, we wanted to do some of the things that had brought joy to them, as well as the entire family. We decided to hold family gatherings and other activities yearly. We felt it was important for our children to get to know their extended family and other relatives. We also wanted them to know their heritage and family history.

To symbolize the coming together of our family, we felt it would be great to have the necklace repaired, keep it as a memento, and use it as part of our celebrations. The beads were stashed away in my closet at that time. They still needed to be restored.

Since the jewelry store in Franklin had been closed for many years, the beads were taken to a local silver shop where they were polished and their natural beauty restored. They were strung in the very same pattern as Mama had always done. A shiny new clasp held them together. The necklace was just beautiful.

Special holidays made us want to be together as a family. So, we decided to come together each year on Thanksgiving Day, an idea Rebie had initiated several years earlier. That seemed to work fairly well, and most family members made special efforts to attend. During those celebrations, we shared family stories, historical information about our ancestors or experiences, and achievements of family members, especially the young people.

Prior to the family gathering in 2010, we decided the necklace was too special to be put away as a family keepsake. It became a symbolic part of the yearly celebration. To honor Mama and Daddy and the strength and values they instilled in us, we decided someone in the family should wear it. Since all of us could not wear it at the same time, we agreed that one daughter would wear it for a year or until the next family gathering. Each year thereafter on Thanksgiving Day or at other family gatherings, the necklace would be passed from one daughter to another— beginning with the oldest.

Since Elizabeth had passed, Ruby was first to wear the necklace. After a brief statement about its origin and importance, it was presented to her. A year later, it was Rebie's turn to wear it.

I was so excited when it was my turn to wear the necklace. By that time, my hair was becoming gray, and the necklace complemented many of the colors I wore. I purchased a special pair of earrings to match it. A picture of my wearing it was placed on my piano. No money is stashed away there. That tradition was not continued.

The year that I kept the necklace passed too quickly. I wasn't ready to pass it to Minnie but couldn't deprive her and the rest of my sisters of the opportunity to wear it. I could've kept it forever. The pride that I felt when wearing it was indescribable. I look forward to wearing it again.

I can't imagine Mama ever felt that a Mason jar containing tarnished beads would become a symbol, which means so much to us long after her death or that its contents could become a keepsake for generations to cherish. I imagine if it were possible, she would smile and be pleased to know we have preserved something that was so special to her.

Hopefully, the remaining sisters will have an opportunity to wear the necklace. As time passes, we trust that it will remain a family heirloom to be worn proudly by the granddaughters, great-granddaughters, and generations to come. It is also our desire that the memento will continue to serve as a reminder of family values our parents instilled in us and traditions they practiced.

ON OUR OWN

Finally, all of you have unity of spirit, sympathy, love for one another, a tender heart and a humble mind.
1 Peter 3:8-9

The death of our parents within a short time was devastating for us. Even though they had experienced health problems for several years, and we realized that no one lives forever, the emptiness was difficult for us to endure. Being the pillars and foundation of the family, they were the force that kept us grounded.

So, what did we do when our circle was broken? Our oldest sister became the matriarch of the family. We relied on her and the guidance we'd gained from our parents and moved forward. I personally remember Daddy's last words, "Y'all take care of yourselves." I've tried to do just that.

Although none of us live in Southampton County, our ties with the area remain strong. For years we visited the area often— sometimes just to visit friends of our parents or the few relatives who live in the area. We continue to visit the family home to make sure it's kept in good condition.

On special occasions, we attend Cedar Grove Baptist Church. Friends and Family Day, which is celebrated there yearly, is important to us because that celebration was initiated by Mama years ago. On that day, each member is encouraged to invite friends and family members to attend morning services. Sometimes, individual families are recognized or asked to take an active part in the celebration.

Dinner is served with much excitement and anticipation. We see and reminisce with folks we grew up with or haven't seen in many years. We also enjoy the food, which is sometimes cooked just the way Mama and the ladies of the church prepared it years ago.

From time to time, we visit the farms where we once lived, sites where the old schools were located, and other areas in the county.

The old schools are still standing although none of them are used for educational activities. Years ago, Rosenwald Elementary and Damascus Elementary were sold and converted to single-family homes. If one looks closely at the buildings, features of the old schools are still visible. A former student keeps the brass school bell from Damascus as a memento.

When schools were consolidated and integrated in the 70s, Hayden High School became a junior high school. After several years, it was closed. Because the school had existed for so long, it was approved for listing in the Virginia Landmark Register in 2012 with plans for renovations and restoration. In 2013, it was added to the National Register of Historic Places.

The farmhouses where we lived no longer exist. During our last visit to the Womble farm, we saw no evidence that the small two-room house at the edge of the farm ever existed. Where the large farmhouse stood, only a portion of one of the barns was visible. Amidst the overgrowth, the pecan trees stood tall— nothing more—no fruit trees or grape arbors. We were told that a huge tree, which grew in the front yard, fell on the house years ago and destroyed the main structure. The yucca plants that grew at the end of the lane during the summer were no longer there. Corn and peanuts were growing in the fields nearby.

It has been almost 50 years since the family left the Beale farm. We were told that the landowner set fire to the farmhouse, barn, chicken coop, and smokehouse. It's not uncommon in rural areas for old buildings to be burned to clear areas for farming. On our last visit, fields of corn covered the entire acreage.

The oak tree, which spread its limbs over the house like a huge umbrella and provided much needed shade on hot days during the summer, is just a memory. So is the cedar tree I transplanted in what was the front yard.

The Scotts continue to own the land adjacent to the farm. Johnny and his wife, Jane, live there and operate a chicken and vegetable farm. We visit them when we're in the area. It's interesting to sit and chat with them—something that we didn't dare attempt many years ago. Because of the segregated society in which we lived at that time, mixing among the races was prohibited. We were young children and had to abide by the laws that existed at that time. We hold no animosity toward them and enjoy our visits but just don't get a chance to do that often.

Members of the Bowers family continue to live on what we called Bumpy Hole Road, which is now officially Bowers Lane, named in honor of the family. We visit them, also. They continue to own and maintain the farm their grandparents acquired years ago. Hearing how Daddy taught farming techniques to some of them brings back memories of life on the farms. I keep in touch with Martha, who lives in Pennsylvania. She recalled going places with us when she lived in the area.

"Although your father usually had a car full of girls, he always made room for me." she said. "I can't forget that."

The Black Creek area looks much like it did years ago although the stores are closed. One store appears to be some type of workshop. Some of the houses remain and look much like they did when we were youngsters. The railroad no longer exists. A pipeline through which water flows from Lake Gaston, NC to Norfolk and surrounding areas has replaced it.

Finding the last farm was not an easy task. I'd completely forgotten how to get there. The family moved there after I left Southampton County. Mama and Daddy didn't live there long, and I never spent much time there. I visited Ruth, who lives not far from the area and asked her to take Eileen and me there.

"Don't you remember how to get there?" she asked.

"I never spent a night on that farm," I said. "I have no idea how to get there."

Since she had lived there longer than any of us, I thought Ruth would know exactly where the farm was located.

After about 15 minutes of driving along winding roads, the car slowed to a stop by a lush soybean field. Near the rear of the field, a cluster of trees jutted out of the nearby woods. I searched for something to convince me that the family once lived there. We saw nothing—no house, no barns. The silo where Daddy stored his grain was also gone.

"Ruth, are you sure this is the farm?" I asked.

"Yes, this is it," Ruth declared. "I know this is where we lived. I remember waiting in this area for the school bus."

Continuing to look, I recognized a magnolia tree towering over the cluster of trees. Remembering the magnolia tree in the front yard let us know where the house once stood. Just like the Womble farm, the forest had completely consumed the area.

As I left the area that day, I experienced a fleeting moment of sadness—concerned that no one lived on any of the farms where we once resided. I took solace, however, knowing the farms continue to exist and are still thriving. The lush fields of corn, soybeans, and peanuts are evidence that tilling the land and caring for the crops continue to be part of someone's journey in life.

Prior to the passing of our parents, all of us left the farms and set out to make homes of our own. Since job opportunities in the county were limited, we did as most young people in the area. We left after completing high school. Trying to find employment in the cities wasn't always easy. Our skills were limited, but the work ethic that we had developed from our parents made an impact. We had also learned not to wallow in self-pity or let our circumstances determine what we would become.

Attending college afforded some of us opportunities to gain additional skills. Others chose positions, which provided on-the-job training. With hard work and perseverance, all of us eventually developed careers, which enabled us to live comfortably and assist with the support of our families.

Looking back today, I realize life for us has gone in ways we didn't expect, and we've had experiences that were never dreamed possible. Our story is probably not much different than other families who lived in the area under similar economic conditions. We're not ashamed of the journey we took to get where we are. We share our plight to reinforce the fact that despite struggles and hardships, it's still possible for success to be attained.

Mindful of our past, we live each day with appreciation for the experiences that shaped our lives and made us who we are today. We credit any success we've attained to Almighty God, lessons from home, the sacrifices of our parents, and support and encouragement from many individuals along the way.

Our journey continues with exciting and challenging experiences. With the dawn of each day, new horizons offer countless possibilities for involvement. We await and embrace whatever the future holds for us.

WHERE ARE THEY NOW?

When people learn that there were nine girls in our family, they want to know more about each of us. What was life like for each of us after leaving Southampton County, VA? What interests do we have today? The question most asked is: where are the sisters now?

Except for Elizabeth who passed in 2007, all of us are retired and live in cities on the East Coast.

Each sister is unique in her own way. As we became adults, our interests evolved. In retirement, we are involved in various ways. Some of us have hobbies that we pursue. We volunteer in our churches and provide much needed services to seniors in our communities. Some of us continue to work part time. Most of us take part in fitness programs. Our children, grandchildren, great-grandchildren, nieces, and nephews keep us busy. We enjoy traveling and being together as a family.

Elizabeth lived in Norfolk, VA, until her death from heart failure and renal disease. Having received training as a certified nurse assistant, she held positions with local hospitals and health-care agencies. Two daughters, Joyce and Alfreda, one son, Michael, six grandchildren, and three great-grand children survive her.

Elizabeth enjoyed growing houseplants. With plants in every room, her place sometimes resembled a greenhouse. She also collected antiques. She frequented local thrift shops, flea markets, and yard sales to add to her collection.

Ruby can be described as the fashionista of the family. She loves to shop for the latest styles, especially hats and shoes. A widow, she lives in Virginia Beach, VA. She is retired after many years from the US Postal Service in Norfolk, VA. An avid walker, she can be spotted daily at the park near her home.

Her humble dedication to her church and community is evident through participation in various ministries and Bible study fellowships. She also volunteers in nursing facilities with the Citizens Committee For the Protection of the Elderly.

She has two sons, James Jr. and William, and one daughter, Sherri. She also has four grandchildren and two great-grandchildren.

Rebie resides in Gainesville, FL, with her husband, Charles. After retiring from the US Postal Service in Washington, DC, and Charles' retirement from the US Department of Defense in Maryland, they chose to spend their retirement years in Florida. They have one son, Charles Anthony, and two daughters, Anita and Tracy. They also have three grandchildren and seven great-grandchildren.

Rebie is active in her church where she serves as a deaconess and participates in the hospital, home, and prison ministries.

The culinary specialist and gardener in the family, she makes the best sweet potato pies and pound cakes in the world. She also has the most beautiful flowers in her neighborhood. She inherited Mama's green thumb. Given a twig or sprig from most plants, she can transplant them and make them grow.

Minnie lives in Mount Vernon, NY. After obtaining an Associates Degree in home economics from Norfolk Division of Virginia State College, now Norfolk State University, she moved to White Plains, NY, where she lived prior to moving to Mount

Vernon. A retired US Postal Service Supervisor, she spends most of her time volunteering in her church, writing poetry, making crafts, and sewing. Since retiring, Minnie has received advanced degrees in theology. Having recently begun studying how to paint with oils, she may be the future artist in the family—a Grandma Moses perhaps. She has one daughter, Angela.

Ernell also resides in Mount Vernon, NY, with her husband, Samuel. They are also retirees from US Postal Service. They have three daughters, Liza, Sharon, and Tanya, and three grandchildren. Ernell is active in her church, where she is a member of the Gospel Choir. She enjoys making crafts for all occasions. She also designs and makes costume jewelry. She and Minnie can usually be spotted participating in many of the arts and crafts shows held in Westchester County, NY.

Eileen joined the Job Corps after high school and received training in Maine. Upon completing a stint with the corps, she found employment in Boston, MA, and lived there for more than 40 years. After working in the bookbinding industry and in security for chipmaker Analog Devices, she desired to be closer to family members. In 2011, she retired and moved to Norfolk, VA, where she resides today.

During her spare time, she volunteers at facilities for senior citizens. She values her Christian upbringing and admonishes family members and others to do likewise.

Yvonne may be described as the most adventurous. She lives in Atlanta, GA, but has also lived in New York, Wisconsin, and Maryland. She likes to travel and has seen more of the world than the rest of us. She enjoys collecting ethnic art and artifacts, which she displays throughout her home.

After completing Norfolk State University, Yvonne held positions with the US Navy in Norfolk, VA, and Crystal City, VA. She is retired after more than 30 years with International Business Machines (IBM). She is a licensed real estate agent and works part time for Cobb County Georgia Public Schools.

Ruth resides in Suffolk, VA, with her husband, Dwight. She is retired after more than 30 years with International Paper. She continues to be a member of Cedar Grove Baptist Church, where she sings in the choir and is a faithful volunteer. Being the youngest, she has all of to look up to. She continues to work part time but enjoys traveling with family and friends. She has two children, Cetina and Brian. She also has four grandchildren.

ABOUT THE AUTHOR

Daphne Harris Dews lives in Virginia Beach, VA, with her husband, James. She is retired after 37 years with Norfolk Public Schools, Norfolk, VA, as an elementary school teacher, reading specialist, and parent-involvement specialist. She is a member of the Virginia Beach Writers Group, which has been in existence for many years and offers support for writers of all genres. With many childhood memories, she enjoys recounting and writing about those experiences. She is a 1964 graduate of Norfolk Division of Virginia State College, now Norfolk State University, with a BS degree in elementary education. Advanced studies were done at Old Dominion University, Norfolk, VA, where she received an MS degree in education in 1985.

Daphne continues to serve her church and community. A member of The Historic First Baptist Church, Norfolk, VA, she participates in Seniors in Action and has assisted with the tutorial program sponsored by the church. Ready Academy, the church-sponsored school, has benefitted from her efforts to assess student progress. Her civic duties have included serving as an election official for the City of Virginia Beach and Chief Election Official for the voting precinct in her neighborhood.

Daphne enjoys traveling and spending time with family and friends. She has two daughters, Satonya and Stephanie.

CREDITS

All photos are from the Harris family's personal collection.

Scripture quotations are taken from the *Holy Bible*, New Living Translation, copyright © 1996, 2004, 2007 by Tyndale House Foundation. Used by permission of Tyndale House Publishers, Inc., Carol Stream, Illinois 60188. All rights reserved.

Page 110, **COME TO JESUS / I WILL TRUST IN THE LORD**, by Reverend Edward Payson Hammond, 1831to 1910.

Page 111,**TAKE ME TO THE WATER,** Traditional Arranged by NINA SIMONE,
© 1967(Renewed), EMI WATERFORD MUSIC and ROLLS ROYCE MUSIC CO.
All Rights Controlled and Administered by EMI WATERFORD MUSIC INC.
Exclusive Print Rights Controlled and Administered by ALFRED MUSIC.
All Rights Reserved. Used By Permission of ALFRED MUSIC.

CPSIA information can be obtained
at www.ICGtesting.com
Printed in the USA
FSOW01n1453300117
30092FS